OATH TAKERS

L. DOUGLAS HOGAN

Copyright © 2015 Douglas Hogan
No part of this book may be reproduced in any manner
whatsoever without permission except in the case of brief
quotations embodied in critical articles or reviews.

All rights reserved.
ISBN: 10: 1508447462
ISBN-13: 978-1508447467

DEDICATION

This book is dedicated to the American oath taker, wherever he or she may be. It was written for you, my brothers and sisters of the Oath. Our mutual pledge to this country and its Constitution is to forever uphold its truth that all men are created equal and are given natural rights. Our pledge to this ideal binds us and reveals in us the true character of America.

ACKNOWLEDGMENTS

I would like to acknowledge my wife, Andrea, who continually encouraged me more than she knows; my brother, James, who regularly lit the fire in me by proposing ulterior views that pushed me back to the keyboard time and time again; my best friend of the '90s, Jason, who helped to teach me commitment and has himself remained as faithful and true to his oath as I have; G. Michael Hopf, best-selling author of the post-apocalyptic New World series, for inspiring me into believing that it's possible to achieve a dream; my mom, Patty, and an innumerable multitude of friends and associates for continuous encouragement; and certainly not last, the Lord Jesus for making this country possible and putting within myself, and every oath taker, specific skill sets and ideals of commitment designed to maintain a free country.

CONTENTS

FOREWARD	vi.
PROLOGUE	1
THE OATH	5
ON OUR FORM OF GOVERNMENT	7
ON SECURING AND PRESERVING ITS CONTENTS	11
REGULATION NATION	13
A CLOSE CALL	22
CONTEXTITUTION	25
U.S. CONSTITUTION	46
JUSTICE SHOULD BE BLIND & LADY LIBERTY'S EYES ARE DIM	74
OF WOLVES AND MEN	82
ORGANIZING	87
RUMORS AND PETITIONS	99
OF MORAL CLARITY	102
FIRST FREEDOM	106
EXECUTIVE ORDERS AND THE CONSTITUTION	110
RACISM AND LIBERTY	113
CONTRASTING A DIVIDED AMERICA	121
FROM THE BOTTOM UP	135
WE NEED YOUR SUPPORT, ARMY, NAVY, AIR FORCE AND MARINES	166
SOME FINAL THOUGHTS ON DEMOCRACY	176
THE COCKROACH THEORY	179
ADDENDUMS	183
LEADERSHIP IN DIFFICULT TIMES	185
PROFESSIONALISM IN DIFFICULT TIMES	187
MINEFIELDS	189
EPILOGUE	191
ABOUT THE AUTHOR	194

FOREWORD

When I received the request from my longtime friend Doug Hogan to write the foreword for his first book, I was a little surprised. Who asks someone who is neither eminent in any field nor well known to write the foreword for their very first book? The point of this thing is, after all, to whet the potential reader's appetite and to draw them into the book, and let's be honest, that is done more often than not by hooking you, the reader, with the celebrity status of the person who wrote it! As I thought about it, however, I realized that this is typical Doug.

Douglas Hogan doesn't really do anything in his life for recognition. There's really no reason to believe that his first book would be any different. Douglas Hogan invests himself heavily into everything he does, and everything he does is done for other people, and that's a fact. In any case, he wasn't looking for a celebrity to do this, but rather, for the very type of person he wants to communicate with through this book: An average American and an Oath Taker.

In the two-plus decades that I've known Doug, he's been many things. What I've noticed about him though, is that just about everything he's done (both personally and professionally) has prepared him with a wealth of experience with which to write this book.

Douglas is a U.S. Marine. I say *"is"* because as any Marine will tell you, once you earn that title you're always a Marine. The Marine Corps is actually where I met Doug more than twenty years ago. Like a lot of Marines, I'd say most Marines in fact, he wasn't there for an easy ride and he surely wasn't there to get rich. No, Douglas Hogan is a patriot and at the time, he saw the Corps, as the best way available to him, to serve the nation and the people he loves. He is the epitome of the Marine Corps motto: Semper Fidelis. He has always been, and (I truly believe) will always be, faithful.

Douglas is also a police officer; out on the streets and doing a job that most of us would rather not have to do, usually while you and I are safe and warm in bed. Doug is the cop that you want to interact with (if you have to at all). He was the guy behind the badge who is concerned about **your rights** as an American citizen far more than he is concerned with writing a ticket or making an arrest.

Above all, though, Douglas Hogan is a family man. Why does that qualify him to write this book? Well, being a family man myself, I know what a powerful motivator it can be. In fact, there really isn't a better reason I can think of for a man to want to ensure prosperity and security for his country than to be able to pass something worthwhile on to his children.

Douglas has spent his entire adult life serving his countrymen. During that time he has come to realize what many of us are aware of as well:

At no time in our American history has our nation ever been in greater danger than that in which we find ourselves now. Integrity seems to be all but gone at every level of government. The bulwarks that have sustained the separation of powers within the various branches of the federal government have been chipped away at until we can almost watch them crumbling before our eyes. Social issues are the hot-topics of the day throughout government at every echelon of government, but the attention is paid to those societal concerns at the expense of the national economy, foreign affairs, and our own national security.

The result is a nation in trouble. The real threat is not external however; there are no hordes massing outside the borders (at least no organized ones), no armies on the march, no coalitions arrayed against us. The threat is far more subtle and far more deadly to us as a nation than those things. The real threat to America today is apathy. Apathy caused by moral decay, by fear, and by frustration. Apathy brought on by a feeling of being powerless to stem the tide. But it isn't over yet.

What you have here, my fellow Patriot is a book written by the average American for the average American. This book is a call to return to our American roots; to remember our heritage and birthright. Most importantly, it is a reminder that our oaths are binding, and we have a responsibility to ourselves and our posterity to honor them. Douglas Hogan writes in a style that is both direct and candid. No words are minced; there is no "beating around the bush" or "tip-toeing through tulips". Douglas says what he means, and his incredible passion is ample evidence that he means what he says.

It's typical Doug.

- Jason Tibbet GySgt, USMC (ret)

PROLOGUE

"I have sworn upon the altar of God, eternal hostility against every form of tyranny over the mind of man." —Thomas Jefferson

Our Constitution has been under attack in recent years. It has been called "outdated" and "obsolete." There are those in both the front lines and in the rear disregarding their oath and the meaning of our Constitution. Whether it's out of ignorance, or if there's a much more sinister reason, it has to stop. The freedoms of every individual in America is at stake.

I am a U.S. Marine, a law enforcement officer, and a security guard. I've been married for twenty-two years and have two children. I have spent the last twenty-plus years serving my country in various capacities. I am a man who loves his nation and holds true to its core documents and the deep abiding principles for which they stand.

I have struggled, in my own way, to keep up the fight and to protect the precious assets of the doctrines in the U.S. Constitution and the context in which they were written. There are two documents in my life that have guided me in the making of good moral judgments and in keeping of good moral values: the Constitution and the Bible; the former being a document written on the foundations of the latter.

Let me premise this note by saying I am not come to convert you to Christianity through this book. I have deep Christian foundations and am a minister of the Gospel of Jesus Christ, but this is about our future as Americans, and I will be focusing on the issues that undermine our Constitution. I will be addressing the oaths taken by those who defend our America. Those of you who serve on the front lines of oblivion; that place where light collides with darkness; where good is versus evil. That place where the very best of America meets the very worst. I want to address issues within our country that cause great rifts between ideologies that threaten our way of life. I want to call out every American that has ever sworn an oath. You know who you are and I want to make sure that you have not, or will not lose your way, and if you have, you do not embody the American spirit but have become a part of the problem that is afflicting our country. Return to the path, and walk the trails that have been tread before you. They are the paths that our forefathers blazed. The paths that rooted themselves in tyranny and government overreach but blossomed into Liberty trees through the shedding of blood, sacrifice, and all manner of selflessness.

The threat this country faces is greater than any foreign invader. It is greater than any military of any land. It is a force equal to that of a great pendulum swinging in the opposite direction. This pendulum is one that threatens America's existence. The scariest part: it swings within the nation itself. Our nation is waning as the pendulum begins its descent in the opposite direction with a force equal to its opposite.

I have identified several factors precipitating the downward spiral in which we find our country falling. Each of these factors, I will break down into topics. The nature in which these topics will be addressed is dependent upon you, the reader.

Within these pages, you will find writings on the history of our country, quotes from our forefathers, the documents that govern our existence as Americans, principles of leadership, the subversion of American rights, racism, hard choices, preparedness, and what is expected of an OATH TAKER.

THE OATH

There are various levels of oath takers; some of them hide behind the ones that stand at the gate, while others go out and confront evil. The lawmakers, the law enforcers, the active duty military, the correctional industry, veterans, firefighters, etc. Many have sworn an oath to their countrymen that they will *support and defend* the Constitution of the United States against all enemies, *foreign and domestic*.

Here is a sample oath, most likely the very oath you swore to your country:

"I do solemnly swear (or affirm) that I will support and defend the Constitution of the United States against all enemies, foreign and domestic; that I will bear true faith and allegiance to the same; that I take this obligation freely, without any mental reservation or purpose of evasion; and that I will well and faithfully discharge the duties of the office on which I am about to enter: So help me God."

The Constitution does not "evolve" or take shape. It does not change or bend its ideals to the concepts of a changing America. It is America that is to bend to the writings of the Constitution. It simply *"is,"* and commands great acts and feats to be altered. It cannot be manipulated by an "executive order." It takes much more than the pen of a single person to change its contents. When you swear an oath, it is to the Constitution. It is not to the government or to some other corruptible entity, such as an executive; it is to the Constitution. If you do not agree with the U.S. Constitution, then there are a host of other countries with different founding documents that you may feel more closely aligned to. Furthermore, if you do not agree with the U.S. Constitution, then this book is not written for you. It is written for those who have already sworn an oath. It is also written for the future oath takers of America. If you are cynical towards our Constitution or you feel that it is "outdated" or worthless, I suggest you stop what you are doing and find another topic of interest. May I recommend *A Communist Manifesto* by Karl Marx and Friedrich Engels?

ON OUR FORM OF GOVERNMENT

The Constitution, the Bill of Rights, and the Declaration of Independence hang above my fireplace. I also keep a copy of these articles in my prep bag. They are very dear to me. Not only will I die for their preservation, but I will fight with every fiber in my being to ensure my children and your children grow up with individual freedoms. Not the freedoms elected to them by the majority, or a dictator, of sorts, but individual sovereign freedoms. This is where one may be confused regarding the current status of the United States.

Our country is currently running as a democracy. It is not written into the Constitution as such. This country was forged to be a *republic*. Even our Pledge of Allegiance is *"to the Republic for which it stands"* (referring to the symbol of the U.S. flag). In a republic, the individual American is sovereign to his/her own rights. Rights are vested with each and every individual American, equally. There should be no *democracy* among the citizens of the United States. In a *democracy*, the rights are vested in the majority. Where the majority dictate, the rights of the individuals in the minority do not apply. In a democracy, when the majority says "thus and such shall be your rights," then those are the rights given to you.

Our Constitution contains a Bill of Rights built into it to insure an everlasting individual freedom. This is why it's so important to protect, defend, and preserve the Constitution of the United States. I do not pretend to be a Constitutional professor. I'm not even a Constitutional senior lecturer; history shows that these titles don't mean too much when a country is being managed by educated derelicts with such abbreviations following their names. That's the beauty of the Constitution. It wasn't written by the educated for the educated. It was written by patriots that dreamed about a country where every person could be free from an overreaching government, where the government would be *the people.* It was written by a thirty-three-year-old planter by the name of Thomas Jefferson. The context of the Constitution is in the history of its creation. It was affirmed and voted into writ by a people fresh from the bonds of tyranny. They saw how a king could become corrupted by power and they watched as it happened.

Though years of intercession to the king went unanswered, it became necessary to fight and die for a great cause. The Constitution was written to permanently eradicate tyranny and to give power to the people of its citizenry. It was written in a time where government was not made up of *the people*, but rather a government unto itself that was made up of people, but not *for the people* or *by the people*. Therein lay the corruptibility of the government. It was through this avenue that the people of the American colonies became victims of their government, and therein lay the reasons the very words were penned:

"When in the Course of human events, it becomes necessary for one people to dissolve the political bands which have connected them with another, and to assume among the powers of the earth, the separate and equal station to which the Laws of Nature and of Nature's God entitle them, a decent respect to the opinions of mankind requires that they should declare the causes which impel them to the separation." —The Declaration of Independence, July 4th, 1776

The oath you swore was to the Constitution. It

was not to an evolving form of government. Over the past several decades, a representative democracy has been the norm, but it was not so in the beginning. One of the greatest concerns during the early convention meetings was securing individual freedoms. Therein is the importance of the Bill of Rights. There will be more on that later, but our oaths are to those laws of the Constitution that give rights to sovereign Americans. As oath takers, your job is to ensure that these rights are kept within the confines of the Constitution and not usurping it. It is to make sure no person, foreign or domestic, tramples them. This defense mechanism was built into the Constitution.

ON SECURING AND PRESERVING ITS CONTENTS

One method utilized for the preservation of the Constitution is called the Oath of Office. The oath of office dates back to the First Congress of 1789. Of course, the original oath was reserved for the President. Article II Section 1(8) of the Constitution reads:

"I do solemnly swear (or affirm) that I will faithfully execute the Office of President of the United States, and will to the best of my Ability, to preserve, protect and defend the Constitution of the United States."

This oath was later adapted for use in other offices within the United States. The adaptation has been modified through the years. Each time it was done, it was done so with the intention of relieving the States of tyranny and traitors of various sorts. The Civil War saw the most adjustments to the oath. The oath of office is specific to those who choose to subjugate themselves to it. From the time you swear the oath until your death, the oath should be alive in you. There is never an undoing or a time that the oath doesn't apply. The patriot makes this pledge, to live and to die therein. Choices made later and to the contrary are betrayal.

We now live in an era where a person "progresses" into more liberal viewpoints and patriotism is subverted into something else. It is now used as a derogatory word to describe people who believe in their individual sovereign rights. Sadly, there are those serving in public office, under oath, calling Americans with guns "domestic terrorists." Those are the activist politicians pushing gun-control agendas. They find themselves in a conundrum on the opportunity to seize Americans' firearms, because they know what it would mean. They feel secure making such decisions behind the mantle of America's military. As if their unconstitutional acts of attrition would be honored by those who have sworn an oath to defend the Constitution, including its Bill of Rights. The very document that grants us our liberties is the same document that binds those in service. Not to the government, but to the Constitution. It binds them to *THE PEOPLE.*

REGULATION NATION

This land has come to a place where it regulates everything the Constitution protects. The lawmakers and various forms of legislators work night and day to restrict liberties that the Constitution gives you. They see the Constitution as a restriction of their intentions, and they are correct in thinking so. It was designed to keep them away.

Today's lawmakers restrict what kind of food you can eat and how much soda you can have. They have written laws infringing your right to keep and bear firearms. They tax your own property and seize your livestock. Virtually every aspect of your life is regulated by an overreaching government. Your job, as an oath taker, is to reject these types of laws. Any law written to violate the rights of another are unconstitutional. Who does the government use to enforce these unconstitutional laws? They use you, the oath taker. The man and woman in uniform. The very person who vowed to uphold the Constitution is the person assigned to undermine it. They come to count on your service to the government to enact their unconstitutional demands. But what if you refuse? What if you can see it for what it is? What if you see political agendas and corruption instead of constitutional parameters? What if every American stopped acting against the Constitution? There are a few questions here and some pretty tough questions to follow. With tough questions come even tougher decisions.

As a police officer, I swore the oath. Daily I see opportunities that beckon me to enforce the government's will upon the people. Daily, I must choose which rights are constitutional and which are violations. To make things clear, let me use an example and illustrate how this thought process works for me.

On a routine day, I see numerous people driving their commute from point A to point B. Daily I see dozens not wearing their seat belt, which the law clearly says must be applied. The dilemma then arises: is it this person's constitutional right to not have to wear a seat belt? Remember the Constitution provides for individual liberties as long as they don't violate the liberties of another.

The person who is not wearing a seat belt is an adult. His death, in the event of an accident, is not for the government to dictate. It is the driver's responsibility to protect himself from harm by fastening his seat belt. It in no way violates the rights of another by his/her refusal to wear a seat belt. The government says he/she is supposed to, but your oath is to the Constitution, not to the government. If no person is at risk, there is no need. If the driver is speeding, the officer should Terry stop him, because his duty is to protect others.

The government has long held the argument that driving is a privilege and not a right. I have a differing view. Under the Fifth Amendment of the Bill of Rights, no person shall be deprived of *liberty* without due process. Within the word *liberty*, you can find almost no boundaries. LIBERTY does not mean anarchy. Your liberty is your own until it violates the liberty of another, and then it becomes unconstitutional. Within the word LIBERTY is *free travel*. Because there is no mention of the word *travel* in the Constitution does not mean it is not your right to travel by horse, train, car, truck, or teleportation at will. The government has found that a silence in the Constitution is a breach in constitutional rights. And where there's a breach, there's a means to CONTROL. In 1770, Thomas Jefferson stated the following while appearing in a court case involving civil liberties: "All men are born free and everyone comes into the world with a right to his own person and using it at his own will. This is what is called personal liberty, and is given him by the author of nature, because it is necessary for his own sustenance."

The government would have you enforce any law where the Constitution is silent. Driving is one such right. The Constitution is silent on driving because there was no such technology at the time. I want to use this as a segue into the Ninth Amendment, which protects rights not specifically mentioned in the Constitution:

The enumeration in the Constitution, of certain rights, shall not be construed to deny or disparage others retained by the people.

Yet in recent times we have seen administrations create legislation where the Constitution is silent, and regulations to existing laws where the law probably should not exist. They (the government) display signs where your constitutional rights do and do not apply, specifically, roping off areas where your First Amendment right to speech applies and where it does not, as was apparent during the Bureau of Land Management's move into Clark County, Nevada, early in 2014. Not even a representative government would conduct such acts of attrition, by fear of having to answer to the people; they write ridiculous laws dictating what the people can eat and drink; they (the government) put signs on public land telling the people they cannot stand on the posted property without the possibility of being arrested for trespassing. All of this dereliction against the American citizen while the southern U.S. Border remains unsecured, with about 10,000,000 illegals living among us with driver's licenses, jobs, health care, and free phones. I say all of this because at the time this chapter was written, our own immigration laws are not being enforced. Immigration control officers are being told to stand down. Men and women sworn to the defense of this country are not keeping to their oath in allowing these people to enter without fear of law. Instead, the focus has shifted to creating legislation against natural-born citizens. We are being tougher on our own law-abiding people than we are active criminality. Taking my son to get a driver's license proved more difficult than an illegal immigrant. I see illegal's with driver's licenses randomly, but don't understand how it can be when my son has to produce umpteenth documents to prove his residence. The police officer should not be bogged down with cumbersome legislation and gray areas.

The suits in Washington, D.C., actively neglect our nation's laws while writing new ones. The highest criminal justice office in the land turns a blind eye to whatever ideology aligns with the administration. This creates a lawless government where fear of accountability is a moot topic. Evidence of criminal activities in the highest offices of the land disappear under subpoena and people refuse to speak before select congressional committees appointed to investigate criminal activities. All the while, the Department of Justice is silent, as if the office is aligned with a political agenda rather than the Constitution of the United States. As a police officer, I have been challenged with directives from political figures to focus on a particular agenda. I am proud to say that upon receiving such orders, I initially dismissed the request to disparage, then after some thought on the matter, I resigned that commission. I have no qualms about submitting a resignation wherever it is due. Foremost, my duties are to my country and the Constitution that governs it, not to the political figures or their agendas. This mind-set should be the norm, not the exception, across the entire spectrum of oath takers, wherever you work, in whatever geographical location, regardless of how seasoned you are. I know that there are certain cultures within the realm of law enforcement, but it's never too late to change for the better, even if it means abandoning that culture for the cause of righteousness. If *we the people* cannot stand for something righteous, then we will fall from the grace of the people of the United States. The people we have sworn to protect and serve.

I can't even begin to cover everything that is regulated in this country. The Illinois Vehicle Code is over 600 pages of regulations. From what color the various lights can be, to the tinting of the windows, to the distance from the ground to the bumper of your vehicle.

If you are reading this, I'm guessing you're interested in politics or you are a person who has taken an oath. I can't say this enough: your oath is to the Constitution. Don't let the government fool you into thinking you are their henchman. You have a choice to enforce the regulations of the land. You are not a state or city thug.

The Constitution is a product of intense debate. A debate that went on for some time in a series of articles known as the Federalist and the Anti-Federalist. The original Constitution did not contain a Bill of Rights, and because of that, there were some who would not sign on to ratify the new Constitution. It wasn't until the Bill of Rights was added, guaranteeing individual sovereign rights, that the last of the delegates signed the Constitution into law. I say this because you are an American first and foremost. More than that, you are an American that has sworn an oath to uphold the Constitution and all its parts, including the Bill of Rights, which provides for the individual citizenry sovereign and inherent rights. The people of America are being regulated to death. Freedom is hemorrhaging out of this country through regulation. You are authorized in the use of officer discretion while on duty. I implore you to act on your oath and make the hard decisions. There may come a time when that decision is more costly than you suspected. At the end of the day you will have maintained your honor. Thomas Jefferson once said, *"The boisterous sea of liberty is never without a wave."* I will close this chapter with another Thomas Jefferson quote: *"I would rather be exposed to the inconveniences attending too much liberty than to those attending too small a degree of it."* Indeed, liberty has its issues, but it's worth the cost.

A CLOSE CALL

I served in the U.S. Marines in the '90s. The period I served in was not without incident, but my unit was not assigned to any foreign excursions. A moment that stands out most, in my mind, was the Los Angeles riots. The Rodney King beatings, perpetrated by white L.A. police officers, sparked widespread riots. The case eventually went to federal courts, where the locals were fearing the worst-case scenario. My unit was briefed on what could repeat itself as another Los Angeles riot event that had occurred the previous year. My greatest fear was being sent into a U.S. city with orders to shoot. The whole briefing was surreal. While I can't recall the information provided or the instruction given, I do recall my only question: "Will we be issued less-than-lethal bullets?" My concern was the use of any method other than lethal. The idea of standing against my own countryman was a dark thing made of nightmares. I can recall the cogs of my mind rotating in a way they were not designed to rotate. The questions couldn't be placed into anything discernible. I understand security. At the time of this book, my security experience spans twenty years. Looking back, I think we were being asked for more than security. We were talking about angry Americans with guns. Angry Americans destroying civil and state properties, burning homes, looting, etc. If security was the assignment, it was about to turn into something far greater. I'm thankful to report, and history will show, that there were convictions on some of those officers. It was enough to appease the potential for violence and to abate the anger of the city. In the spring of 1993, I did not have to point my weapon at a brother American. But more tough decisions were to come later in my life, nothing so intense, but tough, nonetheless.

In 2014, a white Ferguson, MO, police officer shot a large black teenage male. The teen died from multiple gunshot wounds. Those are the facts of the case. Months later, Ferguson remains in a state of riot. I am definitely not a fan of civil disorder, nor am I a proponent of martial law. I have to pass kudos along to Governor Jay Nixon for showing great restraint; however, I am obliged to neutralize that with his comment from a five-minute video on

Ferguson. His second point stated a "vigorous prosecution must now be pursued." Is that where we are as a nation? Where a governor promises the vigorous prosecution of an innocent man? We are still innocent until proven guilty, aren't we? I don't know the guilt or innocence of either man in this case. But the law does. The law says he is innocent until proven guilty. Those calling for the officer's termination and/or conviction must wait until the process has run its course. There is still *due process*, even for the police. No one is convicted or prosecuted without it. Everybody involved in the Ferguson investigation, whether it's defense or prosecution, are sworn to uphold the laws. They cannot circumvent the system for the appeasement of a few clamorous individuals. The loss of liberty starts with a declaration for a little safety and security.

CONTEXTITUTION

The Constitution wasn't just whipped up by free people for free people. There was a gradual worsening of tyrannical prowess in the kingdom of King George III. Many of the same instances we are seeing today. Long before the adoption of the Declaration of Independence, on July 4th, 1776, there were exhaustive attempts at fixing the tyranny problem on every possible level. I stated, towards the front of this book, that I am not a Constitutional professor. It is for this reason I am including various writings, speeches, quotes, excerpts, and documents to aid in the construction of this work. This work is, after all, a book to the oath taker. This chapter is an attempt to bring context into the Constitution for anybody that's interested in knowing why it was framed the way it was and how it applies today. Thus, the title of this chapter is a combination of the two words "context" and "Constitution." What good is it to make my argument without the history to support the context of this work? You swore an oath to defend something worth dying for. Our founders believed this, and those 8,000 American Revolutionaries who gave their lives for liberty certainly believed in the cause. Therefore, to illustrate how desperate the Americans were to resolve the government overreach, I am including Patrick Henry's speech at the Virginia Convention on March 23, 1775. The context is concern for the loss of further liberties. Henry wanted to raise a militia and set a defense. Other delegates wanted to wait and see if the latest petition to the king would work. The following is Patrick Henry's "Give me liberty or give me death" speech. A favorite among present-day patriots.

No man thinks more highly than I do of the patriotism, as well as abilities, of the very worthy gentlemen who have just addressed the House. But different men often see the same subject in different lights; and, therefore, I hope it will not be thought disrespectful to those gentlemen if, entertaining as I do opinions of a character very opposite to theirs, I shall speak forth my sentiments freely and without reserve. This is no time for ceremony. The question before the House is one of awful moment to this country. For my own part, I consider it as nothing less than a question of freedom or slavery; and in proportion to the magnitude of the subject ought to be the freedom of the debate. It is only in this way that we can hope to arrive at truth, and fulfill the great responsibility which we hold to God and our country. Should I keep back my opinions at such a time, through fear of giving offense, I should consider myself as guilty of treason towards my country, and of an act of disloyalty toward the Majesty of Heaven, which I revere above all earthly kings.

Mr. President, it is natural to man to indulge in the illusions of hope. We are apt to shut our eyes against a painful truth, and listen to the song of that siren till she transforms us into beasts. Is this the part of wise men, engaged in a great and arduous struggle for liberty? Are we disposed to be of the number of those who, having eyes, see not, and, having ears, hear not, the things which so nearly concern their temporal salvation? For my part, whatever anguish of spirit it may cost, I am willing to know the whole truth; to know the worst, and to provide for it.

I have but one lamp by which my feet are guided, and that is the lamp of experience. I know of no way of judging of the future but by the past. And judging by the past, I wish to know what there has been in the conduct of the British ministry for the last ten years to justify those hopes with which gentlemen have been pleased to solace themselves and the House. Is it that insidious smile with which our petition has been lately received? Trust it not, sir; it will prove a snare to your feet. Suffer not yourselves to be betrayed with a kiss. Ask yourselves how this gracious reception of our petition comports with those warlike preparations which cover our waters and darken our land. Are fleets and armies necessary to a work of love and reconciliation? Have we shown ourselves so unwilling to be reconciled that force must be called in to win back our love? Let us not deceive ourselves, sir. These are the implements of war and subjugation; the last arguments to which kings resort. I ask gentlemen, sir, what means this martial array, if its purpose be not to force us to submission? Can gentlemen assign any other possible motive for it? Has Great Britain any enemy, in this quarter of the world, to call for all this accumulation of navies and armies? No, sir, she has none. They are meant for us: they can be meant for no other. They are sent over to bind and rivet upon us those chains which the British ministry have been so long forging. And what have we to oppose to them? Shall we try argument? Sir, we have been trying that for the last ten years. Have we anything new to offer upon the subject? Nothing. We have held the subject up in every light of which it is capable; but it has been all in vain. Shall we resort to entreaty and humble supplication? What terms shall we find which have not been already exhausted? Let us not, I beseech you, sir, deceive ourselves. Sir, we have done everything that could be done to avert the storm which is now coming on. We have petitioned; we have remonstrated; we have supplicated; we have prostrated ourselves before the throne, and have implored its interposition to arrest the tyrannical hands of the ministry and Parliament. Our petitions have been slighted; our remonstrances have produced additional violence and insult; our supplications have been disregarded; and we have been spurned, with contempt, from the foot of the throne! In vain, after these things, may we indulge the fond hope of peace and reconciliation. There is no longer any room for hope. If we wish to be free—if we mean to preserve inviolate those inestimable privileges for which we have been so long contending—if we mean not basely to abandon the noble struggle in which we have been so long engaged, and which we have pledged ourselves never to abandon until the glorious object of our contest shall be obtained—we must fight! I repeat it, sir, we must fight! An appeal to arms and to the God of hosts is all that is left us!

They tell us, sir, that we are weak; unable to cope with so formidable an adversary. But when shall we be stronger? Will it be the next week, or the next year? Will it be when we are totally disarmed, and when a British guard shall be stationed in every house? Shall we gather strength by irresolution and inaction? Shall we acquire the means of effectual resistance by lying supinely on our backs and hugging the delusive phantom of hope, until our enemies shall have bound us hand and foot? Sir, we are not weak if we make a proper use of those means which the God of nature hath placed in our power. The millions of people, armed in the holy cause of liberty, and in such a country as that which we possess, are invincible by any force which our enemy can send against us. Besides, sir, we shall not fight our battles alone. There is a just God who presides over the destinies of nations, and who will raise up friends to fight our battles for us. The battle, sir, is not to the strong alone; it is to the vigilant, the active, the brave. Besides, sir, we have no election. If we were base enough to desire it, it is now too late to retire from the contest. There is no retreat but in submission and slavery! Our chains are forged! Their clanking may be heard on the plains of Boston! The war is inevitable—and let it come! I repeat it, sir, let it come.

It is in vain, sir, to extenuate the matter. Gentlemen may cry, Peace, Peace—but there is no peace. The war is actually begun! The next gale that sweeps from the north will bring to our ears the clash of resounding arms! Our brethren are already in the field! Why stand we here idle? What is it that gentlemen wish? What would they have? Is life so dear, or peace so sweet, as to be purchased at the price of chains and slavery? Forbid it, Almighty God! I know not what course others may take; but as for me, give me liberty or give me death!

I feel strongly that in the words of Mr. Henry's speech there was utter desperation. At one point the attorney and politician made the comment that there was no longer *hope*. He spelled it out very explicitly in his speech that there was naught left but to take up arms. They had been pushed into a corner and there was literally nothing left to do but fight. But the question he raised next was "when?" Shall we take up arms now or wait until the people are totally disarmed? There was already chatter that the colonists were weak because the king had soldiers in the homes of the colonists and they were partially disarmed. The people saw and knew what was transpiring in their midst. It was no secret the government wanted its thumb on the people. For the king, it was a matter of control. Controlling the people was the easy part. If you control the land, you control the people by controlling their food. The king had usurped all land unto himself. He believed that everything belonged to him. The quartering of English soldiers in the homes and lands of the colonists guaranteed the king's ownership and proved to the Americans that the king's reach was indeed long. Patrick Henry saw the urgency of the situation as the king's hand was coming into their homes and confiscating their firearms on a whim. Soon, it would be impossible to defend themselves against the king's yoke of tyranny. Soon it would be too late. Now was the time to take action. To wait was to surrender the will to be free. His appeal was to the God of hosts because there was nothing left to do. He knew the colonists could not defeat Great Britain, but the matter was clear.

We fight, we fight! The millions of people, armed in the holy cause of liberty, and in such a country as that which we possess, are invincible by any force which our enemy can send against us...we shall not fight our battles alone. There is a just God who presides over the destinies of nations, and who will raise up friends to fight our battles for us. The battle...is not to the strong alone; it is to the vigilant, the active, the brave.

What a powerful message! And he was right! God raised up an unlikely ally in the fight against tyranny. England's enemy, France. They had a navy and saw in the American colonists a means to defeat England by spreading them thin.

In an attempt to contextualize what was happening in those days, let's lay a little more backdrop to the history that led up to the American Revolutionary War. Prior to 1763, the American colonists were Englishmen and completely loyal to the king of England. England was suffering, financially, from the Seven Years' War (French-Indian War) and needed more resources and money for national reparations. Every citizen of England, and even the king, was subject to a document called the "Magna Carta." The document was signed some 500 years prior by King John and was an agreement between him and the barons of England that no man is above the law. Apparently King John had been breaking the laws of the land and doing whatever he willed. The Magna Carta (Great Document) meant that there would be equal justice in the land ruled by the king. However, King George III began to enforce unjust laws upon the colonists of America. Their taxes were unreasonably high and they were being taxed excessively. That was just the beginning of their woes. After a decade of pleading and petitions to the king, things only became worse as the king became more and more unruly. Things continued to escalate as the American colonists rejected taxation without representation and the authority of parliament. After the Boston Harbor incident, Great Britain attempted punitive actions against the colonists. American colonists then expelled the royal officials that were assigned to America. Not long after that, Great Britain sent soldiers to the colonies to re-establish British rule. The American patriots defeated them and thus began the American Revolutionary War. As time progressed, the newly formed Congress felt the need to make the declaration for independence official. They then drafted the Declaration of Independence in 1776. Within the verbiage of the declaration was a list of unruly behavior by King George III. The list provided in the Declaration of Independence was probably not an exhaustive one, but was a powerful list, nonetheless.

Being ratified on July 4th, 1776, the Declaration of Independence, now solidified as a part of the U.S. Constitution, enumerated many of the tyrannical behaviors of the king and his treatment of the Americans. Read the Declaration and then the list of the king's tyranny. See if you can notice anything correlating to where we are today as a nation. They say history repeats itself. I'm smelling quite a few similarities.

When in the Course of human events it becomes necessary for one people to dissolve the political bands which have connected them with another and to assume among the powers of the earth, the separate and equal station to which the Laws of Nature and of Nature's God entitle them, a decent respect to the opinions of mankind requires that they should declare the causes which impel them to the separation.

We hold these truths to be self-evident, that all men are created equal, that they are endowed by their Creator with certain unalienable Rights, that among these are Life, Liberty and the pursuit of Happiness. That to secure these rights, Governments are instituted among Men, deriving their just powers from the consent of the governed, That whenever any Form of Government becomes destructive of these ends, it is the Right of the People to alter or to abolish it, and to institute new Government, laying its foundation on such principles and organizing its powers in such form, as to them shall seem most likely to effect their Safety and Happiness. Prudence, indeed, will dictate that Governments long established should not be changed for light and transient causes; and accordingly all experience hath shewn that mankind are more disposed to suffer, while evils are sufferable than to right themselves by abolishing the forms to which they are accustomed. But when a long train of abuses and usurpations, pursuing invariably the same Object evinces a design to reduce them under absolute Despotism, it is their right, it is their duty, to throw off such Government, and to provide new Guards for their future security.—Such has been the patient sufferance of these Colonies; and such is now the necessity which constrains them to alter their former Systems of Government. The history of the present King of Great Britain is a history of repeated injuries and usurpations, all having in direct object the establishment of an absolute Tyranny over these States. To prove this, let Facts be submitted to a candid world.

He has refused his Assent to Laws, the most wholesome and necessary for the public good.

He has forbidden his Governors to pass Laws of immediate and pressing importance, unless suspended in their operation till his Assent should be obtained; and when so suspended, he has utterly neglected to attend to them.

He has refused to pass other Laws for the accommodation of large districts of people, unless those people would relinquish the right of

Representation in the Legislature, a right inestimable to them and formidable to tyrants only.

He has called together legislative bodies at places unusual, uncomfortable, and distant from the depository of their Public Records, for the sole purpose of fatiguing them into compliance with his measures.

He has dissolved Representative Houses repeatedly, for opposing with manly firmness his invasions on the rights of the people.

He has refused for a long time, after such dissolutions, to cause others to be elected, whereby the Legislative Powers, incapable of Annihilation, have returned to the People at large for their exercise; the State remaining in the mean time exposed to all the dangers of invasion from without, and convulsions within.

He has endeavoured to prevent the population of these States; for that purpose obstructing the Laws for Naturalization of Foreigners; refusing to pass others to encourage their migrations hither, and raising the conditions of new Appropriations of Lands.

He has obstructed the Administration of Justice by refusing his Assent to Laws for establishing

Judiciary Powers.

He has made Judges dependent on his Will alone for the tenure of their offices, and the amount and payment of their salaries.

He has erected a multitude of New Offices, and sent hither swarms of Officers to harass our people and eat out their substance.

He has kept among us, in times of peace, Standing Armies without the Consent of our legislatures.

He has affected to render the Military independent of and superior to the Civil Power.

He has combined with others to subject us to a jurisdiction foreign to our constitution, and unacknowledged by our laws; giving his Assent to their Acts of pretended Legislation:

For quartering large bodies of armed troops among us:

For protecting them, by a mock Trial from punishment for any Murders which they should commit on the Inhabitants of these States:

For cutting off our Trade with all parts of the world:

For imposing Taxes on us without our Consent:

For depriving us in many cases, of the benefit of

Trial by Jury:

For transporting us beyond Seas to be tried for pretended offences:

For abolishing the free System of English Laws in a neighbouring Province, establishing therein an Arbitrary government, and enlarging its Boundaries so as to render it at once an example and fit instrument for introducing the same absolute rule into these Colonies.

For taking away our Charters, abolishing our most valuable Laws and altering fundamentally the Forms of our Governments:

For suspending our own Legislatures, and declaring themselves invested with power to legislate for us in all cases whatsoever.

He has abdicated Government here, by declaring us out of his Protection and waging War against us.

He has plundered our seas, ravaged our coasts, burnt our towns, and destroyed the lives of our people.

He is at this time transporting large Armies of foreign Mercenaries to compleat the works of death, desolation, and tyranny, already begun with circumstances of Cruelty & Perfidy scarcely paralleled in the most barbarous ages, and totally unworthy the Head of a civilized nation.

He has constrained our fellow Citizens taken Captive on the high Seas to bear Arms against their Country, to become the executioners of their friends and Brethren, or to fall themselves by their Hands.

He has excited domestic insurrections amongst us, and has endeavored to bring on the inhabitants of our frontiers, the merciless Indian Savages whose known rule of warfare, is an undistinguished destruction of all ages, sexes and conditions.

In every stage of these Oppressions We have Petitioned for Redress in the most humble terms: Our repeated Petitions have been answered only by repeated injury. A Prince, whose character is thus marked by every act which may define a Tyrant, is unfit to be the ruler of a free people.

Nor have We been wanting in attentions to our British brethren. We have warned them from time to time of attempts by their legislature to extend an unwarrantable jurisdiction over us. We have reminded them of the circumstances of our emigration and settlement here. We have appealed to their native justice and magnanimity, and we have conjured them by the ties of our common kindred to disavow these usurpations, which would inevitably interrupt our connections and correspondence. They too have been deaf to the voice of justice and of consanguinity. We must, therefore, acquiesce in the necessity, which denounces our Separation, and hold them, as we hold the rest of mankind, Enemies in War, in Peace Friends.

We, therefore, the Representatives of the united States of America, in General Congress, Assembled, appealing to the Supreme Judge of the world for the rectitude of our intentions, do, in the Name, and by Authority of the good People of these Colonies, solemnly publish and declare, That these united Colonies are, and of Right ought to be Free and Independent States, that they are Absolved from all Allegiance to the British Crown, and that all political connection between them and the State of Great Britain, is and ought to be totally dissolved; and that as Free and Independent States, they have full Power to levy War, conclude Peace, contract Alliances, establish Commerce, and to do all other Acts and Things which Independent States may of right do. And for the support of this Declaration, with a firm reliance on the protection of Divine Providence, we mutually pledge to each other our

Lives, our Fortunes, and our sacred Honor.

The Declaration of Independence and the war against Great Britain was done without a government as we know governments. Congress was a body of patriots that levied the war against a tyrannical government. Fifty-four men, representing thirteen colonies, with differing views at almost every angle, except for the cause of LIBERTY, had to work together to secure liberty for this nation we know today. They had different political beliefs, differing religions, were upper classes and lower classes, yet they worked together to secure LIBERTY and to defend against *tyranny*.

Before a Constitution could be drawn up, the States were requested to draft their own Constitutions. While the States were drafting their governments, the Articles of Confederation was drafted. It was the first attempt at building a centralized government. There were widespread disagreements on the issue of slavery.

Slavery existed, but it was contrary to the ideals of freedom. There were some patriots who would not compromise and others who saw the need for freedom universally. Because it was not possible to bring everybody on board with the new government, it was decided to leave the issue of slavery out of the Articles of Confederation. The Articles was only an attempt at setting up a new government. It proved to be inadequate. With independence declared and the war against England won, the time had come to form a centralized government. This WAS NOT a popular topic among the weary war-torn patriots, who had just shaken off a tyrannical government. But they were wise men that understood a lack of centralized government would cause a great deal of perplexities in the future, like war between the States and solidarity in case of foreign invasion. The Constitution was drafted first but could not be ratified because some State delegates refused to sign on because there was no Bill of Rights to guarantee sovereign individual rights. Some believed there was no need for a Bill of Rights because it was believed that the Constitution was sufficient for the preservation of individual rights. Nevertheless, they needed unity between the States and to get that, there needed to be appeasement. It would not be harmful to amend the Constitution to insure such rights would not be infringed. The Bill of Rights was formed and went through a series of adjustments, as did the Constitution as a whole, and was passed in 1789.

THE U.S. CONSTITUTION

(Underscored sections have since been amended or superseded)

We the People of the United States, in Order to form a more perfect Union, establish Justice, insure domestic Tranquility, provide for the common defence, promote the general Welfare, and secure the Blessings of Liberty to ourselves and our Posterity, do ordain and establish this Constitution for the United States of America.

Article. I.

Section. 1.

All legislative Powers herein granted shall be vested in a Congress of the United States, which shall consist of a Senate and House of Representatives.

Section. 2.

The House of Representatives shall be composed of Members chosen every second Year by the People of the several States, and the Electors in each State shall have the Qualifications requisite for Electors of the most numerous Branch of the

State Legislature.

No Person shall be a Representative who shall not have attained to the Age of twenty five Years, and been seven Years a Citizen of the United States, and who shall not, when elected, be an Inhabitant of that State in which he shall be chosen.

<u>Representatives and direct Taxes shall be apportioned among the several States which may be included within this Union, according to their respective Numbers, which shall be determined by adding to the whole Number of free Persons, including those bound to Service for a Term of Years, and excluding Indians not taxed, three fifths of all other Persons.</u> The actual Enumeration shall be made within three Years after the first Meeting of the Congress of the United States, and within every subsequent Term of ten Years, in such Manner as they shall by Law direct. The Number of Representatives shall not exceed one for every thirty Thousand, but each State shall have at Least one Representative; and until such enumeration shall be made, the State of New Hampshire shall be entitled to chuse three, Massachusetts eight, Rhode-Island and Providence Plantations one, Connecticut five, New-York six, New Jersey four, Pennsylvania eight, Delaware one, Maryland six, Virginia ten, North Carolina five, South Carolina five, and Georgia three.

When vacancies happen in the Representation from any State, the Executive Authority thereof shall issue Writs of Election to fill such Vacancies.

The House of Representatives shall chuse their Speaker and other Officers; and shall have the sole Power of Impeachment.

Section. 3.

The Senate of the United States shall be composed of two Senators from each State, <u>chosen by the Legislature</u> thereof, for six Years; and each Senator shall have one Vote.

Immediately after they shall be assembled in Consequence of the first Election, they shall be divided as equally as may be into three Classes. The Seats of the Senators of the first Class shall be vacated at the Expiration of the second Year, of the second Class at the Expiration of the fourth Year, and of the third Class at the Expiration of the sixth Year, so that one third may be chosen every second Year; <u>and if Vacancies happen by Resignation, or otherwise, during the Recess of the Legislature of any State, the Executive thereof may make temporary Appointments until the next Meeting of the Legislature, which shall then fill such Vacancies.</u>

No Person shall be a Senator who shall not have

attained to the Age of thirty Years, and been nine Years a Citizen of the United States, and who shall not, when elected, be an Inhabitant of that State for which he shall be chosen.

The Vice President of the United States shall be President of the Senate, but shall have no Vote, unless they be equally divided.

The Senate shall chuse their other Officers, and also a President pro tempore, in the Absence of the Vice President, or when he shall exercise the Office of President of the United States.

The Senate shall have the sole Power to try all Impeachments. When sitting for that Purpose, they shall be on Oath or Affirmation. When the President of the United States is tried, the Chief Justice shall preside: And no Person shall be convicted without the Concurrence of two thirds of the Members present.

Judgment in Cases of Impeachment shall not extend further than to removal from Office, and disqualification to hold and enjoy any Office of honor, Trust or Profit under the United States: but the Party convicted shall nevertheless be liable and subject to Indictment, Trial, Judgment and Punishment, according to Law.

Section. 4.

The Times, Places and Manner of holding Elections for Senators and Representatives, shall be prescribed in each State by the Legislature thereof; but the Congress may at any time by Law make or alter such Regulations, except as to the Places of chusing Senators.

The Congress shall assemble at least once in every Year, and such Meeting shall <u>be on the first Monday in December</u>, unless they shall by Law appoint a different Day.

Section. 5.

Each House shall be the Judge of the Elections, Returns and Qualifications of its own Members, and a Majority of each shall constitute a Quorum to do Business; but a smaller Number may adjourn from day to day, and may be authorized to compel the Attendance of absent Members, in such Manner, and under such Penalties as each House may provide.

Each House may determine the Rules of its Proceedings, punish its Members for disorderly Behaviour, and, with the Concurrence of two thirds, expel a Member.

Each House shall keep a Journal of its Proceedings, and from time to time publish the same, excepting such Parts as may in their

Judgment require Secrecy; and the Yeas and Nays of the Members of either House on any question shall, at the Desire of one fifth of those Present, be entered on the Journal.

Neither House, during the Session of Congress, shall, without the Consent of the other, adjourn for more than three days, nor to any other Place than that in which the two Houses shall be sitting.

Section. 6.

The Senators and Representatives shall receive a Compensation for their Services, to be ascertained by Law, and paid out of the Treasury of the United States. They shall in all Cases, except Treason, Felony and Breach of the Peace, be privileged from Arrest during their Attendance at the Session of their respective Houses, and in going to and returning from the same; and for any Speech or Debate in either House, they shall not be questioned in any other Place.

No Senator or Representative shall, during the Time for which he was elected, be appointed to any civil Office under the Authority of the United States, which shall have been created, or the Emoluments whereof shall have been encreased during such time; and no Person holding any Office under the United States, shall be a Member of either House during his Continuance in Office.

Section. 7.

All Bills for raising Revenue shall originate in the House of Representatives; but the Senate may propose or concur with Amendments as on other Bills.

Every Bill which shall have passed the House of Representatives and the Senate, shall, before it become a Law, be presented to the President of the United States; If he approve he shall sign it, but if not he shall return it, with his Objections to that House in which it shall have originated, who shall enter the Objections at large on their Journal, and proceed to reconsider it. If after such Reconsideration two thirds of that House shall agree to pass the Bill, it shall be sent, together with the Objections, to the other House, by which it shall likewise be reconsidered, and if approved by two thirds of that House, it shall become a Law. But in all such Cases the Votes of both Houses shall be determined by yeas and Nays, and the Names of the Persons voting for and against the Bill shall be entered on the Journal of each House respectively. If any Bill shall not be returned by the President within ten Days (Sundays excepted) after it shall have been presented to him, the Same shall be a Law, in like Manner as if he had signed it, unless the Congress by their Adjournment prevent its Return, in which Case it shall not be a

Law.

Every Order, Resolution, or Vote to which the Concurrence of the Senate and House of Representatives may be necessary (except on a question of Adjournment) shall be presented to the President of the United States; and before the Same shall take Effect, shall be approved by him, or being disapproved by him, shall be repassed by two thirds of the Senate and House of Representatives, according to the Rules and Limitations prescribed in the Case of a Bill.

Section. 8.

The Congress shall have Power To lay and collect Taxes, Duties, Imposts and Excises, to pay the Debts and provide for the common Defence and general Welfare of the United States; but all Duties, Imposts and Excises shall be uniform throughout the United States;

To borrow Money on the credit of the United States;

To regulate Commerce with foreign Nations, and among the several States, and with the Indian Tribes;

To establish an uniform Rule of Naturalization, and uniform Laws on the subject of Bankruptcies throughout the United States;

To coin Money, regulate the Value thereof, and of foreign Coin, and fix the Standard of Weights and Measures;

To provide for the Punishment of counterfeiting the Securities and current Coin of the United States;

To establish Post Offices and post Roads;

To promote the Progress of Science and useful Arts, by securing for limited Times to Authors and Inventors the exclusive Right to their respective Writings and Discoveries;

To constitute Tribunals inferior to the supreme Court;

To define and punish Piracies and Felonies committed on the high Seas, and Offences against the Law of Nations;

To declare War, grant Letters of Marque and Reprisal, and make Rules concerning Captures on Land and Water;

To raise and support Armies, but no Appropriation of Money to that Use shall be for a longer Term than two Years;

To provide and maintain a Navy;

To make Rules for the Government and Regulation of the land and naval Forces;

To provide for calling forth the Militia to execute the Laws of the Union, suppress Insurrections and repel Invasions;

To provide for organizing, arming, and disciplining, the Militia, and for governing such Part of them as may be employed in the Service of the United States, reserving to the States respectively, the Appointment of the Officers, and the Authority of training the Militia according to the discipline prescribed by Congress;

To exercise exclusive Legislation in all Cases whatsoever, over such District (not exceeding ten Miles square) as may, by Cession of particular States, and the Acceptance of Congress, become the Seat of the Government of the United States, and to exercise like Authority over all Places purchased by the Consent of the Legislature of the State in which the Same shall be, for the Erection of Forts, Magazines, Arsenals, dock-Yards, and other needful Buildings;—And

To make all Laws which shall be necessary and proper for carrying into Execution the foregoing Powers, and all other Powers vested by this Constitution in the Government of the United States, or in any Department or Officer thereof.

Section. 9.

The Migration or Importation of such Persons as any of the States now existing shall think proper to admit, shall not be prohibited by the Congress prior to the Year one thousand eight hundred and eight, but a Tax or duty may be imposed on such Importation, not exceeding ten dollars for each Person.

The Privilege of the Writ of Habeas Corpus shall not be suspended, unless when in Cases of Rebellion or Invasion the public Safety may require it.

No Bill of Attainder or ex post facto Law shall be passed.

No Capitation, or other direct, Tax shall be laid, <u>unless in Proportion to the Census or enumeration herein before directed to be taken.</u>

No Tax or Duty shall be laid on Articles exported from any State.

No Preference shall be given by any Regulation of Commerce or Revenue to the Ports of one State over those of another: nor shall Vessels bound to, or from, one State, be obliged to enter, clear, or pay Duties in another.

No Money shall be drawn from the Treasury, but in Consequence of Appropriations made by Law; and a regular Statement and Account of the

Receipts and Expenditures of all public Money shall be published from time to time.

No Title of Nobility shall be granted by the United States: And no Person holding any Office of Profit or Trust under them, shall, without the Consent of the Congress, accept of any present, Emolument, Office, or Title, of any kind whatever, from any King, Prince, or foreign State.

Section. 10.

No State shall enter into any Treaty, Alliance, or Confederation; grant Letters of Marque and Reprisal; coin Money; emit Bills of Credit; make any Thing but gold and silver Coin a Tender in Payment of Debts; pass any Bill of Attainder, ex post facto Law, or Law impairing the Obligation of Contracts, or grant any Title of Nobility.

No State shall, without the Consent of the Congress, lay any Imposts or Duties on Imports or Exports, except what may be absolutely necessary for executing it's inspection Laws: and the net Produce of all Duties and Imposts, laid by any State on Imports or Exports, shall be for the Use of the Treasury of the United States; and all such Laws shall be subject to the Revision and Controul of the Congress.

No State shall, without the Consent of Congress,

lay any Duty of Tonnage, keep Troops, or Ships of War in time of Peace, enter into any Agreement or Compact with another State, or with a foreign Power, or engage in War, unless actually invaded, or in such imminent Danger as will not admit of delay.

Article. II.

Section. 1.

The executive Power shall be vested in a President of the United States of America. He shall hold his Office during the Term of four Years, and, together with the Vice President, chosen for the same Term, be elected, as follows

Each State shall appoint, in such Manner as the Legislature thereof may direct, a Number of Electors, equal to the whole Number of Senators and Representatives to which the State may be entitled in the Congress: but no Senator or Representative, or Person holding an Office of Trust or Profit under the United States, shall be appointed an Elector.

<u>The Electors shall meet in their respective States, and vote by Ballot for two Persons, of whom one at least shall not be an Inhabitant of the same State with themselves. And they shall make a List of all the Persons voted for, and of the Number of Votes</u>

for each; which List they shall sign and certify, and transmit sealed to the Seat of the Government of the United States, directed to the President of the Senate. The President of the Senate shall, in the Presence of the Senate and House of Representatives, open all the Certificates, and the Votes shall then be counted. The Person having the greatest Number of Votes shall be the President, if such Number be a Majority of the whole Number of Electors appointed; and if there be more than one who have such Majority, and have an equal Number of Votes, then the House of Representatives shall immediately chuse by Ballot one of them for President; and if no Person have a Majority, then from the five highest on the List the said House shall in like Manner chuse the President. But in chusing the President, the Votes shall be taken by States, the Representation from each State having one Vote; A quorum for this Purpose shall consist of a Member or Members from two thirds of the States, and a Majority of all the States shall be necessary to a Choice. In every Case, after the Choice of the President, the Person having the greatest Number of Votes of the Electors shall be the Vice President. But if there should remain two or more who have equal Votes, the Senate shall chuse from them by Ballot the Vice President.

The Congress may determine the Time of chusing the Electors, and the Day on which they shall give their Votes; which Day shall be the same throughout the United States.

No Person except a natural born Citizen, or a Citizen of the United States, at the time of the Adoption of this Constitution, shall be eligible to the Office of President; neither shall any Person be eligible to that Office who shall not have attained to the Age of thirty five Years, and been fourteen Years a Resident within the United States.

<u>In Case of the Removal of the President from Office, or of his Death, Resignation, or Inability to discharge the Powers and Duties of the said Office, the Same shall devolve on the Vice President, and the Congress may by Law provide for the Case of Removal, Death, Resignation or Inability, both of the President and Vice President, declaring what Officer shall then act as President, and such Officer shall act accordingly, until the Disability be removed, or a President shall be elected.</u>

The President shall, at stated Times, receive for his Services, a Compensation, which shall neither be encreased nor diminished during the Period for which he shall have been elected, and he shall not receive within that Period any other Emolument from the United States, or any of them.

Before he enter on the Execution of his Office, he shall take the following Oath or Affirmation:—"I do solemnly swear (or affirm) that I will faithfully execute the Office of President of the United States, and will to the best of my Ability, preserve, protect and defend the Constitution of the United States."

Section. 2.

The President shall be Commander in Chief of the Army and Navy of the United States, and of the Militia of the several States, when called into the actual Service of the United States; he may require the Opinion, in writing, of the principal Officer in each of the executive Departments, upon any Subject relating to the Duties of their respective Offices, and he shall have Power to grant Reprieves and Pardons for Offences against the United States, except in Cases of Impeachment.

He shall have Power, by and with the Advice and Consent of the Senate, to make Treaties, provided two thirds of the Senators present concur; and he shall nominate, and by and with the Advice and Consent of the Senate, shall appoint Ambassadors, other public Ministers and Consuls, Judges of the supreme Court, and all other Officers of the United States, whose Appointments are not herein otherwise provided for, and which shall be established by Law: but the Congress may by Law vest the Appointment of such inferior Officers, as they think proper, in the President alone, in the Courts of Law, or in the Heads of Departments.

The President shall have Power to fill up all Vacancies that may happen during the Recess of the Senate, by granting Commissions which shall expire at the End of their next Session.

Section. 3.

He shall from time to time give to the Congress Information of the State of the Union, and recommend to their Consideration such Measures as he shall judge necessary and expedient; he may, on extraordinary Occasions, convene both Houses, or either of them, and in Case of Disagreement between them, with Respect to the Time of Adjournment, he may adjourn them to such Time as he shall think proper; he shall receive Ambassadors and other public Ministers; he shall take Care that the Laws be faithfully executed, and shall Commission all the Officers of the United States.

Section. 4.

The President, Vice President and all civil Officers of the United States, shall be removed from Office on Impeachment for, and Conviction of, Treason, Bribery, or other high Crimes and Misdemeanors.

Article III.

Section. 1.

The judicial Power of the United States, shall be vested in one supreme Court, and in such inferior Courts as the Congress may from time to time ordain and establish. The Judges, both of the supreme and inferior Courts, shall hold their Offices during good Behaviour, and shall, at stated Times, receive for their Services, a Compensation, which shall not be diminished during their Continuance in Office.

Section. 2.

The judicial Power shall extend to all Cases, in Law and Equity, arising under this Constitution, the Laws of the United States, and Treaties made, or which shall be made, under their Authority;—to all Cases affecting Ambassadors, other public Ministers and Consuls;—to all Cases of admiralty and maritime Jurisdiction;—to Controversies to which the United States shall be a Party;—to Controversies between two or more States;—<u>between a State and Citizens of another State,</u>—between Citizens of different States,—between Citizens of the same State claiming Lands under

Grants of different States, and between a State, or the Citizens thereof, and foreign States, Citizens or Subjects.

In all Cases affecting Ambassadors, other public Ministers and Consuls, and those in which a State shall be Party, the supreme Court shall have original Jurisdiction. In all the other Cases before mentioned, the supreme Court shall have appellate Jurisdiction, both as to Law and Fact, with such Exceptions, and under such Regulations as the Congress shall make.

The Trial of all Crimes, except in Cases of Impeachment, shall be by Jury; and such Trial shall be held in the State where the said Crimes shall have been committed; but when not committed within any State, the Trial shall be at such Place or Places as the Congress may by Law have directed.

Section. 3.

Treason against the United States, shall consist only in levying War against them, or in adhering to their Enemies, giving them Aid and Comfort. No Person shall be convicted of Treason unless on the Testimony of two Witnesses to the same overt Act, or on Confession in open Court.

The Congress shall have Power to declare the

Punishment of Treason, but no Attainder of Treason shall work Corruption of Blood, or Forfeiture except during the Life of the Person attainted.

Article. IV.

Section. 1.

Full Faith and Credit shall be given in each State to the public Acts, Records, and judicial Proceedings of every other State. And the Congress may by general Laws prescribe the Manner in which such Acts, Records and Proceedings shall be proved, and the Effect thereof.

Section. 2.

The Citizens of each State shall be entitled to all Privileges and Immunities of Citizens in the several States.

A Person charged in any State with Treason, Felony, or other Crime, who shall flee from Justice, and be found in another State, shall on Demand of the executive Authority of the State from which he fled, be delivered up, to be removed to the State having Jurisdiction of the Crime.

<u>No Person held to Service or Labour in one State, under the Laws thereof, escaping into another, shall, in Consequence of any Law or Regulation</u>

<u>therein, be discharged from such Service or Labour, but shall be delivered up on Claim of the Party to whom such Service or Labour may be due.</u>

Section. 3.

New States may be admitted by the Congress into this Union; but no new State shall be formed or erected within the Jurisdiction of any other State; nor any State be formed by the Junction of two or more States, or Parts of States, without the Consent of the Legislatures of the States concerned as well as of the Congress.

The Congress shall have Power to dispose of and make all needful Rules and Regulations respecting the Territory or other Property belonging to the United States; and nothing in this Constitution shall be so construed as to Prejudice any Claims of the United States, or of any particular State.

Section. 4.

The United States shall guarantee to every State in this Union a Republican Form of Government, and shall protect each of them against Invasion; and on Application of the Legislature, or of the Executive (when the Legislature cannot be convened), against domestic Violence.

Article. V.

The Congress, whenever two thirds of both

Houses shall deem it necessary, shall propose Amendments to this Constitution, or, on the Application of the Legislatures of two thirds of the several States, shall call a Convention for proposing Amendments, which, in either Case, shall be valid to all Intents and Purposes, as Part of this Constitution, when ratified by the Legislatures of three fourths of the several States, or by Conventions in three fourths thereof, as the one or the other Mode of Ratification may be proposed by the Congress; Provided that no Amendment which may be made prior to the Year One thousand eight hundred and eight shall in any Manner affect the first and fourth Clauses in the Ninth Section of the first Article; and that no State, without its Consent, shall be deprived of its equal Suffrage in the Senate.

Article. VI.

All Debts contracted and Engagements entered into, before the Adoption of this Constitution, shall be as valid against the United States under this Constitution, as under the Confederation.

This Constitution, and the Laws of the United States which shall be made in Pursuance thereof; and all Treaties made, or which shall be made, under the Authority of the United States, shall be the supreme Law of the Land; and the Judges in every State shall be bound thereby, any Thing in the Constitution or Laws of any State to the Contrary notwithstanding.

The Senators and Representatives before mentioned, and the Members of the several State Legislatures, and all executive and judicial Officers, both of the United States and of the several States, shall be bound by Oath or Affirmation, to support this Constitution; but no religious Test shall ever be required as a Qualification to any Office or public Trust under the United States.

Article. VII.

The Ratification of the Conventions of nine States, shall be sufficient for the Establishment of this Constitution between the States so ratifying the Same.

The Word, "the," being interlined between the seventh and eighth Lines of the first Page, The Word "Thirty" being partly written on an Erazure in the fifteenth Line of the first Page, The Words "is tried" being interlined between the thirty second and thirty third Lines of the first Page and the Word "the" being interlined between the forty third and forty fourth Lines of the second Page.

THE BILL OF RIGHTS

The U.S. Bill of Rights

The Preamble to The Bill of Rights

Congress of the United States begun and held at the City of New-York, on Wednesday the fourth of March, one thousand seven hundred and eighty nine.

THE Conventions of a number of the States, having at the time of their adopting the Constitution, expressed a desire, in order to prevent misconstruction or abuse of its powers, that further declaratory and restrictive clauses should be added: And as extending the ground of public confidence in the Government, will best ensure the beneficent ends of its institution.

RESOLVED by the Senate and House of Representatives of the United States of America, in Congress assembled, two thirds of both Houses concurring, that the following Articles be proposed to the Legislatures of the several States, as amendments to the Constitution of the United States, all, or any of which Articles, when ratified by three fourths of the said Legislatures, to be valid to all intents and purposes, as part of the said Constitution; viz.

ARTICLES in addition to, and Amendment of the Constitution of the United States of America, proposed by Congress, and ratified by the Legislatures of the several States, pursuant to the fifth Article of the original Constitution.

Note: The following text is a transcription of the first ten amendments to the Constitution in their original form. These amendments were ratified December 15, 1791, and form what is known as the "Bill of Rights."

Amendment I

Congress shall make no law respecting an establishment of religion, or prohibiting the free exercise thereof; or abridging the freedom of speech, or of the press; or the right of the people peaceably to assemble, and to petition the Government for a redress of grievances.

Amendment II

A well regulated Militia, being necessary to the security of a free State, the right of the people to keep and bear Arms, shall not be infringed.

Amendment III

No Soldier shall, in time of peace be quartered in any house, without the consent of the Owner, nor in time of war, but in a manner to be prescribed by law.

Amendment IV

The right of the people to be secure in their persons, houses, papers, and effects, against unreasonable searches and seizures, shall not be violated, and no Warrants shall issue, but upon probable cause, supported by Oath or affirmation, and particularly describing the place to be searched, and the persons or things to be seized.

Amendment V

No person shall be held to answer for a capital, or otherwise infamous crime, unless on a presentment or indictment of a Grand Jury, except in cases arising in the land or naval forces, or in the Militia, when in actual service in time of War or public danger; nor shall any person be subject for the same offence to be twice put in jeopardy of life or limb; nor shall be compelled in any criminal case to be a witness against himself, nor be deprived of life, liberty, or property, without due process of law; nor shall private property be taken for public use, without just compensation.

Amendment VI

In all criminal prosecutions, the accused shall enjoy the right to a speedy and public trial, by an impartial jury of the State and district wherein the crime shall have been committed, which district shall have been previously ascertained by law, and to be informed of the nature and cause of the accusation; to be confronted with the witnesses against him; to have compulsory process for obtaining witnesses in his favor, and to have the Assistance of Counsel for his defence.

Amendment VII

In Suits at common law, where the value in controversy shall exceed twenty dollars, the right of trial by jury shall be preserved, and no fact tried by a jury, shall be otherwise re-examined in any Court of the United States, than according to the rules of the common law.

Amendment VIII

Excessive bail shall not be required, nor excessive fines imposed, nor cruel and unusual punishments inflicted.

Amendment IX

The enumeration in the Constitution, of certain rights, shall not be construed to deny or disparage others retained by the people.

Amendment X

The powers not delegated to the United States by the Constitution, nor prohibited by it to the States, are reserved to the States respectively, or to the people.

JUSTICE SHOULD BE BLIND AND LADY LIBERTY'S EYES ARE DIM

"The rifle itself has no moral stature, since it has no will of its own. Naturally, it may be used by evil men for evil purposes, but there are more good men than evil, and while the latter cannot be persuaded to the path of righteousness by propaganda, they can certainly be corrected by good men with rifles."
—*Jeff Cooper,* **Art of the Rifle**

It becomes painfully sorrowful for me to admit that we are seeing many of the same "usurpations" in our day that the American patriots saw in their day. The events, names, and dates have changed, but tyranny, in its essence, cannot be disputed by any person with clear sight. With the United Nations putting pressure on an easily impressionable leftist agenda to abolish the 2nd Amendment of the U.S. Constitution, it becomes clear that we are nearing the possibility of a second American revolution. The Bill of Right's Second Amendment is the one remaining guarantee to a free world. The freedom is world renowned and has done its part to secure our borders since 1776. The late Japanese emperor was quoted as saying that he would never invade the United States because there would be an armed American behind every blade of grass. The terrorist caliphate known as "ISIS," in all their ignorance and delusions of grandeur, have stated that they will not rest until they have raised their flag over the White House. What they fail to understand is that the American spirit is unbreakable. It is our freedom that Americans fight and die for. They do the same in the name of their religion, but there is a difference. Freedom is given by God and it cannot be converted. It cannot be converted to a democracy, or to a socialist state, or to communism. That is the natural order and sequence that would evolve if it were not for fighters and defenders of freedom. This country was formed as a republic. It has begun its evolution onto the slippery slope of democracy, and now we are seeing its foothold in socialism as the government pushes its citizens into dependency upon the very system that fools it into thinking it's providing security. This security under the guise of protecting its people by withholding a little freedom. Let us not forget the quote of Benjamin Franklin: *"Those who would give up essential liberty to purchase a little temporary safety, deserve neither liberty nor safety."* This quote is a stark reminder that giving up liberty in the name of safety is the catalyst to losing all liberty, eventually. It comes in the name of "safety." Gun control comes in the name of "safety." While blind Americans seek to abolish their own right in order to bring a little temporary safety, sinister ideals are waiting in the background to strike while the iron is hot. "In the name of safety," they will cry.

Then when the 2nd Amendment is gone, so are your liberties, all of them. None of this happens suddenly, but slowly and methodically the pieces are put together. It's like a giant puzzle without a box cover. You see the pieces coming together, but you can't make out exactly what it is you're looking at. So is the slow and methodical disintegration of a nation of free people. And so, what can be done? That is the big question that we ask ourselves. At least those who can see well enough to discern what is happening. There needs to come a moment in time when *we the people* say enough is enough. But what will be the catalyst? What will be the proverbial "straw" that breaks the camel's back? What of the proverbial "things must come to a head"? What is the answer, and who will lead the charge?

It is my opinion that, excluding the involvement of an outside entity, the striking of the 2nd Amendment will be that catalyst. I continually see the regulating of firearms and ammunition. These regulations appear to be spearheaded by large liberal city politicians; nevertheless, the fight for these freedoms is an ever-present engagement as the National Rifle Associations. continually engages the leftist agenda in our courts. Sometimes the people win, and sometimes there's another erosion. To me, the Constitution is clear. It specifically reads that the right of the people to keep and bear arms *shall not be infringed*. In other words, shall have *no boundaries*. It seems pretty clear to me that the Constitution preserves this right for the individual American and that the right is intended to be without limitation or regulations. The systematic shredding of this right slowly ebbs away the right to possess at all. But suddenly a court case is won that "allows" us to carry concealed as long as we meet the regulations that are set. This victory makes us feel happy and content, but the truth of the matter is, we have lost. If the right to bear arms is regulated at all, then it has been infringed. If it has been infringed, then why all the celebration? The loss of freedoms give rise to celebration when a regulated right has been given back to the people.

It can be compared to taxation. When you have earned a series of paychecks throughout the year and it has been taxed into oblivion, you feel happy at the end of the tax season because you have received a tax "credit." The government took most of it, then gave back a small portion of it, giving you the sensation of a victory when all the while, they still have a third of your payday. And so, when the government says you cannot carry concealed, and later it is determined that, yes, you can, but it must be regulated, you are elated to have won the right to carry concealed, and you don't consider the fact that your right has been infringed. This slow transition from undisputed and unequivocal right to keep and bear arms to loss of liberty is done ever so slowly and methodically that the common citizen is lulled into it without recognizing the telltale signs of it while it is occurring.

So if the catalyst for change is the loss of the one and only liberty that secures the entire Bill of Rights, and it happens in such a small scope that it's barely recognizable as happening, how can it be considered a catalyst for change? If the people are waiting for the government to go door knocking, confiscating guns, they are mistaken. If that were to happen, that would certainly be a catalyst. But the dissolution of the first freedom will most likely come by another means. The leftist agenda will square with any opportunity to make it happen, unless it impedes or interferes with their individual agenda. For example, the United Nations has been pushing gun control treaties on the U.S. for some time.

I recently read a report that Secretary of State John Kerry signed a small arms ban that is supposed to control the amount of firearms that terrorists get their hands on. The more sinister plan, in my opinion, is to control weapons worldwide, thus barring the Bill of Right's 2nd Amendment. If the left and other gun-control activists in government can use such an instrument to bring about an end to their means without it interfering in their future in politics, they would. The barrier, thus far, is the equalization of power between the Executive, Judicial, and Legislative branches of government. Prior to the 2014 mid-term elections, the House of Representatives was controlled by Republicans, the Senate was controlled by Democrats, and the

Judicial are appointments. The Affordable Care Act (ObamaCare) was pushed through with a destabilization of power, by the Democrats controlling both the House and Senate. Could such a destabilization of power occur again where gun control could be pushed through without enough elected opposition to stop it?

To change the Constitution is no simple task. It was designed in such a way that it has to be passed by the Executive, House of Representatives, Senate and approved by two-thirds of the States. What bizarre circumstances would have to be in place to bring about such a thing? I'm not sure and not much given to conspiracy theories, but I do know that I want to be prepared for the time my country will need me. One thing I can't deny, and that is the fact that regulations could very well do the job. If they've come this far and have not been seriously challenged for regulating us to death, how far will it go? And what of foreign policies? Are we beyond the possibility of being attacked on a more devastating level than that of 9/11? Is the genre of post-apocalyptic books and stories beyond the realm of possibilities? What about the "prepper" TV shows and survival guides?

I am inclined to believe that Americans can sense something is amiss and things aren't quite sitting well with them. The economy is in the worst shape it has ever been in and an economic collapse is eminent; the Middle East conflicts are escalating; little is being done to destroy threats to our national security; disasters of biblical proportions are taking place; deadly viruses are being weaponized; the U.S. Constitution is being trampled by elected officials; various offices of the government are lawless; nonmilitary government departments, such as the Bureau of Land Management, are being armed and put against American citizens; the First Amendment is being barred by our government in certain locations; and to top it off, oath takers are becoming lawless. These are just some of the issues plaguing our country. It's time to organize and it's time to be ready. If you are an oath taker, you have a job in securing your country and barring it from anarchy and tyranny, the two extremes we must fight between in order to find balance and liberty.

OF WOLVES & MEN

"A patriot must always be ready to defend his country against his government."
—Edward Abbey

There's no easy way to go about explaining the content of this chapter, but it must be noted that it is the sole purpose of this book, and the total context of its contents. If there's nothing else in this book you will remember, remember the context of this chapter. Not necessarily the contents, but the context.

Most recently, I was engaged in conversation with several people about the current state of our country. We were talking about "preppers"—prepper shows, EMPs, and such—when my friend and author G. Michael Hopf's, **THE NEW WORLD** series came up in conversation. One of my friends spoke up and mentioned that he would be one of the guys plundering to get by. He went on to say that if he knew you, you would be okay, but if he didn't, not so much. We laughed it off, but as time progressed, my mind continued to wonder on it. In fact, I lost some sleep over the matter. Here was my chain of thoughts: This man is a U.S. veteran, one who has served with distinction and honor. He served in the U.S. Marine Corps, where he was trained by the best in the art of warfare. He is a marksman trained in the use of various sorts of weapons, both knives and guns. He swore an oath to protect and defend the Constitution of the United States of America. This oath, being similar to that of a marriage vow, is for better or for worse; for richer, for poorer; in sickness and in health; 'til death do us part. And such was my chain of thoughts. What condition would our nation have to be in for such a person to break an oath to God and country? As I meditated on it, I thought that maybe I had it all wrong. Perhaps the problem wouldn't be vested in the country at all. Perhaps the problem lies in the oath taker. What if something went wrong in the thought process of the veteran? What if the police officer forgets his/her oath? Where would the nation be if every oath taker forgets to be an oath keeper?

There is no end to an oath. There is no time anywhere in the process of retirement, end of active service, or resignation that involves the raising of your right hand and unswearing the oath to the

Constitution. Here's the issue: Supposing the probability for an EMP were likely to happen, or if it did, the need for America's patriots would never be at its highest. With the need for a stabilized and working government absent, in the event of an electromagnetic pulse, the patriot will have to step up in order to fulfill his/her obligation of the oath.

One function of an armed people is to prevent tyranny. Likewise, one function of government is to prevent anarchy. With government out of the equation, anarchy takes root. Anarchy, being the absence of law, is a tree of death. Its fruits are famine, pestilence, tyranny, general lawlessness, threat of invasion, and ultimately, survival of the fittest. Enter the oath keeper. An organized group of men and women with the knowledge and integrity necessary to maintain law and order in an otherwise chaotic situation. Their job is to promote fair trade, free travel, and liberty, without fear of loss of life or limb. They are the post-apocalyptic police. Nightmares are made of military-trained men of war that are trying to save themselves only. The fight-or-flight syndrome is in full effect in a life-or-death situation. Enter the context of this chapter: OATH TAKERS MUST BE OATH KEEPERS!

If you are reading this book, it's likely you picked it up because it caught your eye, being an oath taker. You must prepare yourself for a crisis situation and be prepared for it to happen at any time. The sheep of America are looking for you, the sheepdog, to keep the wolves away! The wolves are out there, and the recent riots in Ferguson, MO, prove that they seek to exploit open windows of opportunity. The wolves are the people of America that seek to take advantage of the weak and unsuspecting citizens of America. Your job, as an oath taker, and hopefully an oath keeper, if I can get you on board, is to be the protector, the guardian at the gate. The watcher who stands guard in the night so the sheep can sleep in peace knowing they are safe. Your job is that of the sheepdog. You have great potential for violence, but your skills have been honed; you have been trained to use them as a force for good. The wolf uses his capacity for violence to commit evil acts against the sheep; but not you. You use your knowledge for good. To maintain a watch, a constant itch that needs to be scratched. It's an itch that never stops itching; it never goes away. Even if you try to put it in the far recesses of your mind, it finds its way back to the forefront and center mass. You long for action. You long for a time your country needs your services.

That time may someday come. It may come in the form of a tyrannical leader or it may come through foreign attack. However it comes, be prepared to act on the side of preserving our way of life; not just any way of life, but the way our forefathers designed it to be. Constitutional restoration will most certainly come at the cusp of a major crisis. When that time comes, sustainability will be the only option until a good functional government can be re-established. America must not be allowed to burn or fall to depravity by the works of wolves and the tree of death.

ORGANIZING

Every man has limits. He has boundaries and walls in his life that not only work to keep things out, but a wise man sets them to keep him from falling over the edge. When I drove home from California after having served four years in the Marines, I made it a point to visit the Grand Canyon. Once there, I noticed the guard rail provided for our safety, designed to keep us from falling over the edge toward certain death. These same safeguards I have put in my life to protect me and my family. I have been a faithful watchman, ever looking for signs of danger and the unseen. So then, in my watchfulness and concern for safety, I have set up certain boundaries and things to watch for in my country, that when those boundaries are crossed, I am to respond. I believe the word is "causality," the relationship between cause and effect. The way causality works is similar to the analogy of the pendulum in the front of this book. To make it more scientific in explanation, Newton's Third Law of Motion is when one body exerts a force on a second body, the second body simultaneously exerts a force equal in magnitude and opposite in direction on the first body. While Newton's laws of motion cannot literally be applied to principles and ideologies, it merits an application because, like Newton's Third Law and the rule of causality, the events and happenings of this world demand an equal regard.

For me, the boundary was the possibility, and potential presidency, of a relatively unknown senator winning the office of the commander in chief of the armed forces of the U.S. My research showed this senator to have no favorable voting record in regards to the 2nd Amendment. I remember visiting voting record websites and doing my homework. As I returned to those sites in the research of this topic, I was unable to find his records. It was as if they had been removed. My research, in totality, showed a man that favored national legislation that would control guns on the state level. Other issues on gun control dealt with bans on manufacturers and concealed-carry permits. I saw radical views in him by the associations he kept. I know that he associated with domestic terrorist Bill Ayers, before he was in public office. I also know that there was a great deal of concern over his citizenship. I came into possession of an early picture of him in Muslim clothing. His pastor was a radical racist and openly preached race hate and politics from the pulpit. All these things and more brought concern to me that our country could vote such a person into the most prestigious position in the free world. Here was a man who did not hold down a single job for more than a couple years, until 1993, when he landed a job at a Chicago law firm, and now he was interested in commanding the armed forces; to me, that was alarming.

I would later learn that command of military forces was not the agenda. Rather, it was a lack of command, in fact, a purge of military command whose views were not aligned with his own. I've seen the list, and it is extensive. I've never felt more powerless than the day Barack Hussein Obama was elected President. When I began writing this book, I had already determined not to make this book a political one. As you read, please try to understand that I am writing from my own perspective, and in doing so, I am laying a groundwork and foundation for this chapter.

I have already mentioned boundaries and the

need to have them. For me, when my spider sense began to tingle, I began researching in depth and continued to be alarmed at how *charisma* could be so powerful a tool to control an electorate. I wasn't affected by the charm and smooth speech. Working in a detention center for years, around the mentally ill and sex offenders, taught me how to build safeguards against being psychologically manipulated by smooth characters. I'm able to detach from human emotion that would otherwise say "things are okay" and turn towards the more sophisticated form of human understanding: logic.

After more than six years, I am all the more convinced that too many Americans have been deceived and convinced of the good fight that Obama presents. For me, the decision to act is based on a series of actions and inactions by this particular administration, whether real or perceived.

To date, nothing has been done to secure our border and address the crisis and the flood of illegal immigrants streaming through it at an alarming rate, despite the 2006 Secure Fence Act. To date, nothing has been done about the Benghazi attack, and the families of the fallen still have zero answers. To date, nothing has been done to bring home

Sergeant Tahmooressi, a U.S. Marine being held in a Mexican prison, despite U.S. Code Title 22, Foreign Relations & Intercourse, Paragraph 1732, which states the U.S. President must act and demand of the foreign government the release of our man. **[UPDATE: Sgt Tahmooressi was released October 31 by a Mexican judge—no thanks to our POTUS.]** To date, there has been no justice for Border Patrol Agent Brian Terry, who fell victim to this administration's Fast & Furious scandal. To date, nothing has been done to the IRS leadership for the systematic targeting of the Associated Press and conservative groups. The reason why these matters have not been addressed is because the highest law enforcement office in the land is not holding true to the oath of office. Instead of appointing external investigators, the AG instead investigates itself and covers its own tracks. The evidence is not swept under the rug, it is destroyed.

In the case of the Lois Lerner emails, the hard disk drive was scratched so severely that it couldn't be read. So, instead of turning the evidence over to a crime lab, the HDD (hard disc drive) was destroyed and recycled so that the evidence would never turn up. So much for the most "transparent administration in history."

Obama has assaulted the Second Amendment with unprecedented abuse of executive orders. On multiple occasions, I've heard receptionists at the doctor's office ask patients if they have guns in their homes. That particular questionnaire is built into the unconstitutional Affordable Care Act. I always refuse to answer it. Obama has made "recess" appointments when Congress was not in recess. He also acted militarily in Libya without congressional approval, despite the authority of the War Powers Act. In a 2014 State of the Union address, Obama alluded to gun-control measures "with or without Congress." How unconstitutional is that?

There comes a point that when a people can no longer trust their government, certain action must be taken. My safeguard is the organization of militia-type groups. While I wait for more desperate actions, I am preparing, rather than sitting idle, for a crisis. My research began with looking up "how to organize a militia." I grew tired of hearing about gun control every time a criminal shot somebody. With the nation turning so far to the left, I decided it was time to organize. To my surprise, I didn't have to start from scratch. I joined up with a large group and eventually took a commission over a large section of Illinois geography.

Dozens of people, veteran and nonveteran, registered with the same concerns that drove me to this point. I scheduled training days, times, places, etc., but eventually found the paranoia of the populace to be a considerable weight. Many were rightfully concerned that the government was spying on them and that no digital media networking was safe. Meetings began on a regular basis, but I soon discovered most of the members just wouldn't show up. People were angry but not desperate enough to organize. This was confounding to me, because I understood the desperate situation America was, and is, in, but was unable to relay the urgency of the situation. Many were paranoid of me because I was a cop and they viewed the police as government thugs. In one particular interview with potential members, I learned that my affiliation with the police made them nervous to join. Maybe it was for the best. Because I don't need members that are worried about the police. That causes me to doubt their legitimacy.

After several failed organization attempts with

use of media, I had a disagreement with the group I was with and broke away. I had several members that wanted to stay under my leadership, and I counted it an honor, but I knew I had quite a bit to deal with and a bunch on my plate. Eventually everything came together and I was able to build a small group without the use of media, but ran into the same issue again. Members were always excited to know what was planned for the next meeting and/or training cycle, but I had the usual handful. Most members just want to be a part of something in case things flush, but don't much want to deal with the hassles of getting ready for said flush. I'm content having a small group, but there needs to be greater organization on a national level.

I see many of the same things our forefathers went through in their day. I see perilous times as our country worsens. I see several years of pleading and petitions that go unheard. I see our rights being trampled under the foot of the government, particularly under the foot of the President. I see a need for a group of delegates to organize a means to an end of tyrannical mismanagement and presidential and congressional usurpation. So many similarities exist now as they did then.

I have taken time out of my schedule to research a greater more organized way to deal with the political corruptions now plaguing our country. I searched around the Internet and stumbled upon U.S. Freedom Army, a group organized by Lewis Shupe, author of the Presidential Diary books, for the purpose of bringing our Constitution back to the people. Several goals are being discussed for the purpose of returning constitutional rights to the people. These goals will be reached in a variety of ways, including marches, petitions, the handing out of flyers, demonstrations, protests, etc. The unconstitutional violations we are currently seeing can be organized under five major areas:

1. Limited Power: These are more specifically referred to as the enumerated powers listed in Article 1 Section 8 of the United States Constitution and buttressed by Amendment X. The continuous violations of the principle of limited government are the greatest threat to your freedom.

2. Separation of Powers: All three branches of government are currently in violation of the separation of powers. The Congress should be making law, the Executive should be enforcing the law, and the Judicial should be interpreting the law. We now have the Executive and Judicial making law and the Congress passing laws they are constitutionally forbidden to pass.

3. Management of the money supply: The United States Constitution requires that all money be backed by some metal such as gold or silver. The abandonment of this standard is a primary reason the debt will ultimately destroy the U.S. economy.

4. Amendment II: The continuous shenanigans used by various government officials to try to disarm the populace must be halted. This would have a higher place were it not for the efforts of the NRA and other concerned citizens.

5. Amendment IV: The warrantless intrusions into the private lives of citizens need to be stopped. It is simple—if you wish to collect information from citizens, obtain a warrant.

The U.S. Freedom Army organization seems to be a pretty well-organized system. It is currently not a militia, but circumstances change. The United

States is full of splintered groups of militias, preppers, and such that need a centralized means of communication and structure. I have found this in the U.S. Freedom Army. I recommend oath keepers and militia leaders register at www.USFreedomArmy.com and do your research. If you are a militia leader, you will maintain almost full autonomy.

I know there are people reading this book that are very nervous about any type of media, for fear of government spying. May I be so bold as to say this country will continue on its present course if you remain in the shadows? We should not be, nay, cannot be afraid of our government! Thomas Jefferson said, *"When government fears the people, there is liberty. When the people fear the government, there is tyranny."* Our Constitution was built within certain defaults to protect us from tyranny. Thomas Jefferson made it clear that it is the right of the people to throw off the government when this happens. In 1792, during George Washington's presidency, Jefferson stated, *"Every people may establish what form of government they please, and change it as they please, the will of the nation being the only thing essential."* How will this government problem get resolved if we stay in the shadows? Or if we continue to hide and communicate our concerns in secret? I started out that way then realized I was sick and tired of whispering. I want to be heard. Edmund Burke said, *"The only thing necessary for the triumph of evil is for good men to do nothing."* The best predictor for future behavior is our history of past behavior. When we see our government heading backwards to a totalitarian government, then the best action is preparedness so that our men and women can answer the call to defend their liberty.

RUMORS & PETITIONS

In some of the research I put into this effort, I discovered several bits of information that I'm glad I fact-checked. I normally catch scuttlebutt on Facebook or Twitter that are just not true. I've fallen victim to these tweets and posts myself, and learned the hard way that research is always the optimal answer prior to the spread of information. I remember one of the hot rumors of the Affordable Care Act was that it did not apply to the President or to Congress. How could anybody know? Nancy Pelosi (representative from California) made the famous comment that if you want to know what's in the bill, you have to pass it first. That's exactly what happened. The bill was pushed through, sometimes under cover of secret legislative assemblies, at times when they were certain there could be no oppositional filibustering. Tyranny is defined as that which is legal for government but illegal for the citizenry (Thomas Jefferson). I believe it was at the passing of the Affordable Care Act that the people began to cry out for a 28th amendment, citing the following:

"Congress shall make no law that applies to the citizens of the United States that does not apply equally to the Senators and/or Representatives; and, Congress shall make no law that applies to the Senators and/or Representatives that does not apply equally to the citizens of the United States." The aforementioned proposed amendment can be petitioned to Washington at **http://www.petition2congress.com/3093/proposed-28th-amendment-to-united-states-constitution/**

Perhaps there's no clause excluding Congress from Obamacare, but there's still a need for such an amendment. I leave that decision to you, but I get nervous at the thought of the Constitution being touched by unruly representatives. Our government has become so corrupt that it conceals its own shortcomings by silence and a lack of transparency to the people. Anytime a congress wants to amend a constitution, there's usually an agenda behind it that doesn't fare favorably for the people. Without a doubt, government has become too large and is destructive to the ends of liberty and the pursuit of happiness. It is therefore the right of the people to abolish such a government and to institute a new government.

"Whenever any form of government becomes destructive of these ends [life, liberty, and the pursuit of happiness] it is the right of the people to alter or abolish it, and to institute new government..." —Thomas Jefferson

"When injustice becomes law, resistance becomes duty."

—Thomas Jefferson

OF MORAL CLARITY

One assumes that a person in uniform is of professional character, undying devotion, compassionate, loyal, has a high aptitude, and is of clear moral character. At least, that is the instructed tradition—there may be a variety of exceptions, depending on the leadership. There are some that pervert our honor system; there are some who slip through the cracks, so to speak; and some outright seek their own ends. I wish I could say that all those in uniform are cut from the same cloth, but I would be deceiving you.

There are some who will agree with me in every topic matter contained in this book, and there are those that will outright disagree with me, maybe even hate me for it. My opinions and views have become more aligned with the old ways than those of the new. I find this happening the more I study our forefathers and take a hard serious look at what we have become as a nation. The moral code was clear when this nation was birthed by the blood of our ancestors. They had very clear moral and ethical Christian values. I find parallels between the work of Christ and the history of the United States. When I place my hand over my heart to speak aloud the Pledge of Allegiance, I do so because in its words are "One Nation under God." I know that I will find moral clarity serving in a nation that is given to "Providence," as the forefathers called it. My mind rehearses the meaning of the flag and what our pledge is about. I must never forget that white stands for moral purity, while the stars (representations of the states) are symbols of heaven, and they remind us of our ultimate goal.

Christ died for humanity that all men might repent and come to the Father through his blood. This act of submission to God and obedience to the gospel brings about spiritual liberty. It is through the shed blood of Christ that all can have liberty. The gospels teach how Christ didn't want to die, but knew there was no other way for man to be brought into the *LIBERTY* He wanted them to have. No wonder the forefathers held this *LIBERTY* so close to their heart. Their nation was one to be built of faith and, though they didn't want to die, it was a sacrifice most worthy. It came by the blood of patriots; and, though they didn't want war, and they didn't want to sacrifice themselves, they saw in their sacrifice a cause worth dying for. This is why it's so important that we, as a nation, cannot forget the sacrifices they made. We cannot become a nation of tyrants, brigands, and thugs! Their sacrifice was to prevent such atrocities.

The code we live by is one of valor, humility, courage, purity of intentions, and selflessness. If we must die, let it be in the name of preserving *LIBERTY*. No oath taker need die in vain; if these traits define you, then you are a patriot. If you have no honor, are haughty, self-oriented, and selfish, you wear the uniform in vain and are a tyrant. You have power that should be used in defense of the Constitution and the people of the United States. When you use those powers for selfish gain or in obedience to a tyrant, you are the tool of tyranny. Alone, a tyrant is powerless, but with arms, legs, and mouthpieces, he controls the masses, because they carry out his will by the use of force. This is why we were given the 2nd Amendment, and why we cannot be free without it.

To you officers of the law, and to you men and women in uniform, under the wing of an executive power, I say this: you must do some serious soul-searching right now. You cannot wait for a moment of clarity when the winds are blowing in a nasty direction; you must have chosen your path before that day comes. Rather, it should have been chosen before you swore the oath. Regardless, a day will come when our nation's patriots are put to the test. A day to follow the order of tyrants, or a day of sacrifice. Nobody wants that day to come, but it has come to every nation of liberty, and we must be fully prepared to make the stand to reinstate the Constitution and to reset the nation of LIBERTY or to stand with tyrants. Both come with sacrifice, but the difference is that of bloodshed by patriots or by tyrants.

L. DOUGLAS HOGAN

FIRST FREEDOM

Our nation's freedom of religious expression has been under direct assault for years. It has been taken to court, shut out of the schools, silenced in institutions, removed from the workplace, and regulated.

Let's discuss these attacks; before we do, let's review the First Amendment:
Congress shall make no law respecting an establishment of religion, or prohibiting the free exercise thereof; or abridging the freedom of speech, or of the press; or the right of the people peaceably to assemble, and to petition the Government for a redress of grievances.

It's pretty clear in its simplicity. The government's not allowed to discriminate or show disparity between religions. Several types of Christian denominations were present at the time of the Constitution's Bill of Rights. Each signer understood the history of having a respect for one religion over another. However, I would like to clear up a misconception that ruled popular opinion for too long. The phrase "separation of church and state" is not in the Constitution. The separation assumed is that Congress shall not respect a certain establishment of religion. In fact, according to the First Amendment, you are allowed to talk about religion anywhere you want. The Amendment clearly says *"Congress shall make no law respecting an establishment of religion, or prohibiting the free exercise thereof; or abridging the freedom of speech."* I can reconcile the phrase "separation of church and state" if the context is that there cannot be a "church-state." A church-state would have essentially re-established a holy empire, similar to that of the tyrannical homeland, from which they had just won their freedom from. No, the First Amendment does not abolish religion from the government or from any workplace. It endorses the free speech of religious topics, encourages the exercise of religion, and shuns the idea of having a church-state; yet the courts continue to hear cases where Americans are offended by the use of religious freedoms and take the exerciser to law.

I think the stupidity started in 1980, in the case Stone vs. Graham, where the Ten Commandments were being purchased with private money and posted as plaques in the school rooms. So long as the students are not required to believe in them or recite them, I fail to see where the violation is. The Commandments weren't purchased with public money, and the students weren't forced to believe in Christian history. Since the plaques were purchased with private money, the freedom of religious exercise was being practiced. However, the courts ruled that the Ten Commandments had no place in the schools.

For years, "evolution" has been taught in our public schools as a matter of fact. Doesn't that show disparity between evolution and creationism? Why is it okay to discriminate against Christians but it's not okay to discriminate against atheism? If atheists don't believe in God, then where is the hurt of having public prayers for those who want to exercise that right? Thomas Jefferson said it best: ***"The legitimate powers of government extend to such acts only as are injurious to others. It does me no injury for my neighbor to say there are twenty gods or no god. It neither picks my pocket nor breaks my leg."*** Christians are passive, for the most part. That's why you don't see widespread riots when they want to make their point known. Instead, they seclude to a place of prayer. If you don't believe in God, that's your prerogative. But if you don't, leave those people who do alone. The Constitution gives them a clear right to exercise their religious preferences.

All the same, the Supreme Court decided a case in 1981 (Widmar vs. Vincent) where the defendant's religious exercises were being excluded by the university. They were not allowing the students to have a religious group. The argument of the State of Missouri and the university was that there should be a separation of church and state. The separation they spoke of was the exclusion clause of the First Amendment. The Supreme Court ruled that they were violating the students' freedom to exercise religious rights. The case set a precedence on First Amendment cases. It clearly defined the meaning of the First Amendment as a freedom to practice religious liberties anywhere. It's not an Amendment that says you can't practice Christianity in the workplace. It is not the "separation of church and state"; it's the "separation of church from state." There is a difference.

EXECUTIVE ORDERS & THE CONSTITUTION

One cannot deny the historical facts that "executive orders" have been a rising trend in the U.S. The usurpation of power and control over every machine designed to bring about the balance of power and control has been the norm and not the exception. Hearing the President mention the use of Executive control if Congress cannot come to agreement, is egregious. Here is the destabilization of power: an extremely left-wing Executive, working with an extremely left-wing Senate, to block bills from the right-wing House, so that an executive order can be passed to promote the socialist agenda. Senator Daniel Webster gave a speech to Congress in 1834, citing that *"the contest, for ages, has been to rescue LIBERTY from the grasp of Executive power."*

Executive orders have been customary since George Washington. Notwithstanding, they are completely unconstitutional. In fact, the Constitution states "All legislative powers herein granted shall be vested in a Congress of the United

States, which shall consist of a Senate and House of representatives" (Article 1 Section 1). Before the Executive takes office, he must swear to faithfully execute those laws—not legislate them.

Executive orders were not originally called "executive orders"; that came later. When Abraham Lincoln was executive, he had every executive order numbered, so that the orders could be tracked. Because executive orders undermine the legislative process, they are nothing short of tyrannical. Most of the early orders were given at times when Congress could not be in session. This is not the case in the current and recent administrations. Congress is very much engaged in the *process,* and the Executive thinks he can trump them with a "pen" and "telephone" (his words).

The late Justice Robert H. Jackson was quoted as saying, ***"Presidential claim to a power at once so conclusive and preclusive must be scrutinized with caution, for what is at stake is the equilibrium established by our constitutional system."*** I'll go a step further and add that a President purposefully cutting out the legislative branch and supplanting it with his own legislation is already a tyrant. We are seeing it as it unfolds before our very eyes. Utter disregard for the Constitution is on the rise, and it has to come to a head. That is the tough question; when is that?

"When the people of America reflect that they are now called upon to decide a question, which in its consequences must prove one of the most important that ever engaged their attention, the propriety of their taking a very comprehensive, as well as a very serious view of it will be evident."

Executive orders expedite the will of the President to advance his personal agenda; and that is tyranny, that is unconstitutional, and a betrayal of the American way of life. It is a betrayal of the Constitution and THE OATH.

RACISM & LIBERTY

Two enigmatic words, *racism* and *liberty*, harmonious and problematic at best. While *liberty* provides for the free expression of one's personal views, it does not provide for unequal treatment of persons of race. Liberty does not discriminate, for it is blind; it does not recognize ethnicity, culture, gender, etc. What liberty does not provide for is the dominion of one person's views over another.

Racism is limited only by a person's ignorance. Plain and simple, racism is hate. It can be taught and it can be learned; it is never natural. Babies, by nature, do not care what color another person may be. It is instilled in them, either through ignorance or brainwash. In the previous baby example, we can learn from the wonders of nature. It can teach us quite a bit. Animals, as another example, do not respond to different colors of the same species (mating rituals being an exception).

Our culture (the human culture) has become very divisive in word and deed. Sometimes an attempt to correct racism ends in a racist action. Words hurt people and many times scars them far beyond their ability to heal, psychologically. This, in turn, breeds animosity, which is reciprocating. It can also be inherent. While I would support intolerance of a tyrannical government, I would not do so where race is concerned. So how can you tell when to be tolerant and when not to be tolerant? The answer is simple. Nature! Nature teaches us that homosexuality is unnatural (a freedom nonetheless). It does not teach us that skin color is unnatural. Nature teaches us that liberty and certain inalienable rights are bestowed to us by our Creator. Therein lies the answer.

What we've been seeing more and more, at an unprecedented level, is the use of race as an excuse to bend the will of the people to that of the race baiter. A *race baiter* has been defined as "an act of using racially derisive language, actions or other forms of communication, to anger, intimidate or incite a person or groups of people, or to make those persons behave in ways that are inimical to their personal or group interests." This can also be accomplished by implying that there is an underlying race-based motive in the actions of others towards the group baited, where none in fact exists. The term "race" in this context can be construed very broadly to include the social constructs which define race or racial difference, as well as ethnic, religious, gender and economic differences. Thus the use of any language or actions perceived to be for the purpose of exploiting weaknesses in persons who can be identified as members of certain groups, or to reinforce a group's perceived victimhood, can be contained within the concept of "race baiting." Many people who practice race baiting often believe in racism or have an interest in making the group believe that racism is what motivates the actions of others.

The term "race baiting" is often a critique of antiracist actions and communications implying that those who criticize apparent racism are themselves guilty of either a form of racism or of simple manipulation. This chapter could be misconstrued as a simple form of racism just because I'm addressing the issue of racism. There are, however, much more complex forms of racism, such as discrimination and institutional racism, which I will go into.

The term "racial discrimination" shall mean any distinction, exclusion, restriction or preference based on race, color, descent, or national or ethnic origin which has the purpose or effect of nullifying or impairing the recognition, enjoyment or exercise, on an equal footing, of human rights and fundamental freedoms in the political, economic, social, cultural or any other field of public life. —UN **International Conventions**

Racial discrimination contradicts the 1776 United States Declaration of Independence, the 1789 Declaration of the Rights of Man and of the Citizen, issued during the French Revolution, and the 1948 Universal Declaration of Human Rights, signed after World War II, which all postulate equality between all human beings.

Racial discrimination is treating people differently through a process of social divisions related to race. Socially acceptable racism seems to include Black Caucuses, Black Commerce, Black Entertainment Television, Black Colleges, Black Scholarships, Black History Months, and Black Marches; probably due to a tragic history of black slavery. It should be noted that the only remnants of this tragic past is the inability to let it be history. It remains in the forward parts of the mind for many people. Even though there are no living slaves in the United States, and no living slave owners, anger and hatred is continually passed along through the generations. Likewise, perceived racial divisions lead to frustrations and violent outbursts that perpetuate the problems of the past. It is these "problems of the past" that lead governments to condone and adopt *institutional racism* as a matter of law.

The term "institutional racism" (also known as "structural racism," "state racism" or "systemic racism") is racial discrimination by governments, corporations, educational institutions or other large organizations with the power to influence the lives of many individuals. Stokely Carmichael is credited for coining the phrase institutional racism in the late 1960s. He defined the term as "the collective failure of an organization to provide an appropriate and professional service to people because of their color, culture or ethnic origin." Obvious guilty parties are noted below.

- The Congressional Black Caucus
- BET (Black Entertainment Television)
- NUE TV (New Urban Entertainment Television)
- Black Family Channel
- The United Negro College Fund (UNCF)
- The National Association for the

Advancement of Colored People (NAACP), etc.

My conservative opinion on affirmative action is that it is the government's answer to correct a wrong with a wrong. The problem with affirmative action is that it can discriminate against a potentially more qualified individual, despite their ethnicity. No person should be given preference based on skin color, whether white or black. The standard should be equality across the board. Providing better instruction on cultural diversity is the answer. Now that we have elected a President who happens to be "black," the problem with affirmative action has escalated. I now feel that my argument against affirmative action is stronger with a "black" President. Here's my rationale:

I don't like the term "African American" because we are "Americans." It is socially divisive to use terminology such as "African American." But, for the purpose of explaining this, we have elected an "African American" to the highest office in the world. It was *not only* "black America" (also divisive) that elected him; ninety-six percent (96%)

of "blacks" voted for Barrack Obama. In a color-blind world, that should have been 50/50, or close to it. Barrack Obama's overwhelming electoral and popular vote means that a consolidated effort of both conservative and liberal efforts won him to be the first "black" President. Undoubtedly, it was nothing less than conservative America that looked through his skin color and saw a man they wanted to fix their national financial crisis. Republican States voted for Obama because they believed his promises. They were unaffected by his ethnicity. He, with the combined effort of the majority of Americans, made his way to the top to get to where he is. He had all the words, and apparently, the right education, to become America's 44th President. That tells me that America is not racist and it's not holding back "black Americans." There is no longer any reason for "white" Americans to feel "guilt" for something their great-great-great-grandfather did wrongly. If "white" Americans voted 96% in favor of the "white guy" the way the "black" community did for Obama, his victory would have been <u>impossible!</u> It's time to dissolve institutional racism. It is unconstitutional and needs to be deleted from our law books as a means to correct a wrong with a wrong.

CONTRASTING A DIVIDED AMERICA

I'm especially sure in today's political queries that you are, at least somewhat, aware of the stark differences between the Republicans' agenda and the Democrats' agenda. Even in today's muddy arena of mud-flinging showdowns, it is becoming more apparent that many political officials are seeing blurry lines between the two political party giants. No matter what political party you feel you are more appropriately aligned with, you still have an obligation to uphold the Constitution.

Wake after wake of controversial topics are overwhelming the most committed politicians. Democrats are leaving the Democratic Party; Republicans are speaking out against their own party. The hate and bitterness are reaching near unprecedented levels. Paint them red or paint them blue, Republican or Democrat, it really doesn't matter what party you claim to be; it all comes down to Liberalism or Conservatism. Politicians tend to paint Conservatives red and Democrats blue. Be it as you will, it really doesn't matter what color you are, the question is, "Are you Liberal or Conservative?" Are you upholding *LIBERTY* or are you dismantling it?

There are many political stances that would render you a Democrat and others that would render you a Republican. Issues that split the two giants are domestic policies, foreign policies, defense issues, abortion, gun control, gay marriage, and the economy. These issues can be divided into three primary categories: national, civil and moral. These issues are the backbone of party issues.

For the purpose of this chapter, I would like to step away from two of these issues and focus on moralism. An idea, I think, America is slipping away from. I'm under the awareness that morality dictates virtually every aspect of life. The absence of morality causes a tailspin that slings out anything that's not grounded. Two major political powers are tearing this country apart by their differing views and polarizing issues. But, specifically, it's not the party names that's causing all the ruckus. It's the morality that ushers in ideology within the parties. Moral groups are not called Republican or Democrat; they are called Liberal and Conservative. While morality may be fluid, the lack of it is the definition of depravity.

Let's consider this; Liberalism is not necessarily Democratic; and Conservatism is not necessarily Republican. Hang on, I'm building up towards my big spill. There are Liberals in the Republican Party and there are Conservatives in the Democratic Party. Now both sides are swooning at the notion that, like Roosevelt's term of office, an unwelcome party has infiltrated political lines. It's not like that! Keep reading.

A political party is objective. They are material organizations to which you must be a registered member. It is, in a sense, an object of attention. This is not the case with Liberalism and Conservatism. These two things are not political parties. It is nothing you can register into. They are subjective. They are philosophies, ethics, values, principles, ideologies, and moralities. They differ depending on the person to whom they are a part of. They evolve as the person evolves. They are subject to the individual and are, in many cases, the product of the environment in which they were raised.

Now, let's expand the scope a little bit. Earlier I basically said that Liberalism and Conservatism were codes of conduct. Let me suggest to you that they are states of mind, if you will. One state of mind is that of high moral clarity and ethics. The other is a separate set of rules that apply to the individual. It is a sense of feel-goodism, or the quick and easy path (the dark side). One is selfishness and the other is selflessness. One says, "I'll take what I can get," whether it's for political gain or for the individual's desire, and the other says, "That is not ethically and/or morally correct." An opportunist will almost always be Liberal.

Another type of person that will almost always be Liberal is the pacifist, but only if others are involved and there is no stake involved on their part. A pacifist that is pacifying for his own sake is not a Liberal but a Conservative. Whereas, a pacifist that is pacifying when something larger than himself is at stake is a Liberal. Liberalism was exemplified in the Liberals lack of concern in the growing threat of the Red Curtain, that is to say the Communist threat of the mid-century. Nothing was done for the better part of twenty years; therefore, the threat grew. Liberal ideology was that the United States was in no "imminent" danger. Thus pacifying the Communist threat until America was living in fear of annihilation. It was conservative values that caused the Red Curtain to fall. Why? Because somebody understood that pacifying evil will only enlarge evil's boundaries. It must be destroyed in its tracks.

We are seeing the same thing with the current threat known as ISIS (Islamic State of Iraq and Syria). The Obama administration has been pacifying the terrorists because they feel that they are no "imminent" threat to the United States. They maintain this view until the threat has grown and become a legitimate and imminent threat to the United States. Now, they are beheading Americans, crucifying children and burying them alive, burning caged people and animals, because the threat was allowed to grow and embolden itself.

The nature of Conservatism is to pacify others when they are the issue, but pacification against large legitimate threats is not how Conservatives deal with them. They understand that the threat is a menace to the liberty of America. The Liberal wants that threat to be ignored until it threatens his individual liberty. When his liberty is then threatened, it becomes paramount to take action. Liberals care little about the liberties of others until their personal liberties are at stake. They would rather not be bothered with the nuances of foreign affairs. The Liberal nature is to indulge themselves and ignore external threats, in the hope they will not become victims. The Liberal will clamor until his/her beliefs are imposed on everybody. The Conservative understands his/her rights are unique to themselves, but will not pacify themselves if it means securing liberty for all; they will sacrifice themselves in a manner exemplified only by patriotism.

Unfortunately, for Liberals, they feel their unique individualism should be forced upon every American. Because the Liberal does not like guns, they push *gun control* upon every American. My personal message to Liberals is, if you don't like guns, don't buy them. When you are experiencing an emergency, wait twenty minutes for the police to arrive. They have guns too, but for some reason, Liberals believe the police and military should be the only ones equipped. That assumption is incorrect, given the Constitution's Bill of Rights has forever given the average American the right to keep and bear arms, in order to secure LIBERTY forever in these States.

No American has the right to impose their belief

system upon that of another. Thomas Jefferson once stated, "Rightful liberty is unobstructed action according to our will within limits drawn around us by the equal rights of others. I do not add 'within the limits of the law' because law is often but the tyrant's will, and always so when it violates the rights of the individual." You heard it here; Thomas Jefferson says that when laws violate the rights of the individual, it is done so by a tyrant.

Let me conclude this chapter by saying all aforementioned Liberal and Conservative chatter was done in order to establish that there are very differing views in this country. The views expressed here are pretty concrete. I understand that there are exceptions in every case. There is a mixture of people, considered "moderates," and also there are exceptions in the ideologies aforementioned. But, for the most part, the views are so contrary that they literally divide America into two categories: Those who seek to undermine and destroy the Constitution's writ of individual liberty and those set to defend LIBERTY at great peril to themselves. Oath takers ought to be on the side set to defend LIBERTY at great peril to themselves. Be liberal, be conservative, with the willingness to die for something greater than yourself. But do it defending the individual liberties of all, so that we can remain American.

DEAR MR. PRESIDENT

I think the following letter should be a required reading for all Presidents
Throughout the pages of this book, I am making every possible effort to reveal truth as it is. I believe that truth is truth and the fact that someone may view truth in a different light does not take away from the fact that truth is unalterable. Truth does not care what race, sex, or ethical background you are. It does not exist within the realm of human perception. It transcends time, culture, ethnicity, and sex. It does not matter how it is viewed, interpreted, or expressed. Therefore, I plan on telling you how it is. How you take it is entirely up to you. It will not be watered down, it will not always feel good, and it certainly will not appeal to "Feel-Gooders."

I define a "Feel-Gooder" as a person who looks for the moment and allows that moment to determine his/her standing on any given issue, despite his/her system of values. It is the person who says to himself/herself, "If it feels good, then do it." Perhaps, for the sake of defining this doctrine, I will refer to the attitude as "feel-goodism."

This attitude is the spirit America is discovering for a second time. Many of you may have experienced it through the Woodstock period. It was a time when peace, love, drugs, and rock-n-roll were all that mattered. It is the spirit that says to our children, "If it is not harmful to others or violating any rules, then do it."

The liberal element of these "children of the flowers" have become scornful and filled with hate through the years. Their hatred has taken them over and now they are teaching America's sons and daughters in the colleges. They teach their point of view and radicalize our sons and daughters. Our kids leave their professors behind and scorn the United States as if they are their professor's champion of all that is good and right. Unfortunately, they are on the left. Their mind's eye has been seared shut and their new attitude is one of "tolerance."

The problem with this attitude is that once a

generation accepts it, the proceeding generation will not only accept the attitude as the norm, but also will undoubtedly add his/her own perception to it. What was tolerance to the preceding generation is no longer tolerance, but the norm. Therefore a new level of tolerance must be created and accepted. With each acceptable state of tolerance, a standard is dropped.

With political correctness on the scene, it has become apparent to many Americans that Constitutional Rights and Constitutional Righteousness have become blurred. What our Founding Fathers held to be "inalienable" suddenly becomes "alterable." And it's all for the purpose of political correctness.

Political correctness is a lot like pepper spray. Not only does it temporarily blind the person it hits, but it also (unavoidably) gets in the eyes of everybody that is in the immediate vicinity, whether you want it there or not.

With political correctness, once a person views something a particular way, the law concerning the view must reflect the new perception of that law. The person, in turn, is blinded to seeing the law as a violation upon his/her rights until it is changed to suit the new point of view. Fellow "Feel-Gooders" now see this with alarming clarity, and they, in turn, become blinded by the same point of view, even if they do not particularly want to view it that way. I guess the issue at hand would be "alternative."

An alternative must now be met for the person who is seeing his/her rights being infringed upon. For political correctness, this person must not be allowed to feel that his/her rights are being violated.

I purposely used the word "alternative" because it's a word that many people these days feel comfortable with. The sad truth is this: alternative is a fancy word for "compromise," which brings uncomfortable feelings of unrighteousness into a person's being. Political correctness says that this person must not be allowed to feel "uncomfortable." Everybody must be appeased so that no particular person feels as though his or her rights are being violated. Suddenly, we see the laws being "redefined" by liberal black-coats. Therefore, we do not have "compromising lifestyles" in America; we have "alternative lifestyles." We do not have "compromised Christian music"; we have "alternative Christian music." We say "alternative" to be politically correct; but let's face the music, it is compromise; and compromise is what's causing our society to degrade with each passing generation.

We hear our parents tell us how things were in their day. Their parents told them similarly. You might tell your kids how things were done in your day. With each passing generation, if you will take the time to consider, society becomes worse and worse. The reason is compromise and tolerance.

It was in my lifetime that homosexuals became openly homosexual. When I was a child, it was taboo. In my parents' time it was almost fictional. In my grandparents' time, it was unheard of. I want to say that, before them, it was nonexistent, though history would prove otherwise.

We see it on television commercials, men and women in their undergarments. This was taboo twenty years ago. The language we hear today on television and on the radio is unlike anything we heard as children. The music we hear today is unlike the music our parents listened to.

Tolerance has a weird way of blinding you to the reality of what's really happening to society. Standards are no longer necessary for social graces. Social graces use to be alive in every aspect of life. Today it is only seen in certain circles, and even then, you had better watch your back.

Concerning political correctness, it is of utmost importance that we exercise extreme caution when trying to make everyone happy. Don't forget that in an attempt to please the new generation, you are abolishing the very standards your parents and your grandparents held so dear. Ask them about their way of life. Not now, but then. They will be the first to tell that so much has changed. Now more than ever, it is detrimental that we hold to the goodness that once thrived in our nation and, may I dare to say, the goodness that originates from the Almighty. Dare I say the "G" word? That's right; the politically incorrect word...GOD! So before you dare to remove "one nation under God" from our pledge to the flag and "In God We Trust" from the face of our currency, all for the purpose of political correctness, try to picture our nation without the God that has given us the rights and the powers we currently enjoy so much. Because you can mark my words, "If you desire the Almighty to take the passenger seat next to political correctness, He will not waste any time leaving, and the beauties you enjoy so much will be lost." And it doesn't bother me to talk about God, because it's my right as an

American. If you don't like me bringing up God in a book, then stop reading. Bottom line is this, political correctness is poison. Political correctness is a violation of the First Freedom; it is a violation of the American way. It says you can no longer use terms like "homosexual" in the workplace. Why? It's because political correctness has entered into bogus ethic reform. While some ethic reform is necessary, certain forms are a violation of my freedom of speech. There's no amendment protecting a person's right from being offended! It's your First Amendment right to express your homosexuality. Be content in that and leave me alone to express my opinion that heterosexuality is natural.

FROM THE BOTTOM UP

Nearly every oath taker began their oath with an act of "initiative." A simple fundamental of leadership. What we have in this country is a degradation of leadership at every level. While I've never served in an elected office, I still have a few words for the officials serving in that capacity. Leadership is not a brand that applies to only one sect of society. It is like liberty in the sense that everybody can enjoy it, and serve it, if it is done right. Leadership can be served at every level. It's not reserved for corporate commandos or military officers. In the military, you are instructed in the fundamentals and principles of leadership at the earliest rank upward. And reflecting on it, I can say that leadership should always be served from the bottom up; not to be confused with management that is dictated from the top down.

Our Congress has lost their way, supplanting the will of the people for their own ideologies. Sadly, the people in office with this mind-set are already below the moral requirement for leadership. It would take a life-changing event to bring a person back from moral depravity to a position of leadership. The reason? Moral depravity is hubris built. A haughty person doesn't want to be humble. "Service" is vaguely defined in their vocabulary. It is beneath them to "serve." They seek only a means to their own desires. Leadership is servant hood, and servant hood is below the proud.

This is why it's important that oath takers be humble in their service. Servant hood is the role of the oath taker. Words like "truth," "faithfully" and "serve" can be found in various forms of oaths. These are *service* words. They bring to thought words like "integrity" and "honor." This is why I'm including a few lessons on LEADERSHIP in this chapter. Your goal, as a servant, is that of a leader, not a manager; and I will explain the difference later, but for now, understand that the oath taker is assuming the position of a leader, and all the respect one would expect of an oath taker to have, is found in *service*, not dictatorial positions of management.

The driving force behind every good leader is good instruction. Like the ol' cliché says, "you are what you eat"! You, as a leader, are a direct product of influence, instruction, and the lessons of life. You have learned from your predecessors and have grafted the traits that best influenced you into your own character. You have received, and are in the process of receiving, instruction that should impact you for the duration of your leadership. Like your character, which is or was a product of your environment, leadership skill is a direct result of impact. Everything the leader does will have a direct impact upon another person, whether for good or for bad. There is no gray area that has a neutral impact on lives. Therefore, the leader must live as if every eye is always upon him. People watch the leader, they hear the leader, and they study the leader. Everything you do, everything you say, every action you take, every response you make; it's all being observed. You are held to a higher standard, because much is vested in you.

The purpose of what I'm writing is not to make you a leader. No book, course, or seminar can make you a leader. Leadership is acquired through many factors. Reading materials and courses are only a couple. Even swearing an oath and taking a position of office or of influence does not make you a leader. The willingness of people to back you and support you through good times and bad is what makes you a leader. The leadership fundamental known as *initiative* is just a building block of leadership. It's a trait, a telltale sign of leadership.

I'm trying to make a substantial contribution to the foundation that has already been laid or is already in the process of being laid. You, as an oath taker, will build upon the foundation and shape your organization, beginning with yourself.
Accepting the fact that you should be serving as a leader isn't always easy to swallow. Especially if you've been elected to be a leader. Many are elected because they have been identified as such. Or perhaps, their **potential** has been identified. Many good leaders are able to identify traits in people that can be fine-tuned. If you have been selected by a leader, such as an officer, executive, or another type of authority, this is probably the case.

To determine if you have been selected as a potential leader, compare yourself to the following:
- I have been asked to fill a position in a lower level of responsibility.
- I have been asked to do a task that requires special trust.
- I have been placed in a position, or asked to

perform a task, that requires competence.
- I have learned servanthood.

The above list is not an exhaustive one, but if you have answered "yes" to any of them, then you have probably been identified as a **potential** leader. Now that you are aware of your potential, allow your leaders to shape you. This will require time and patience. They will shape you by putting more demands upon you. In the process of this period, you may, or may not, find out that perhaps you weren't leadership material after all. There is no shame in that. Many people are better followers than leaders. Continue to support your leaders and grow in the area in which you were planted. You will find, if you haven't already, that it's the "little things" that are every bit as vital as management.

"It's what you learn after you know it all that counts." — John Wooden

Those of you who are actively serving in positions that require leadership should utilize the information in this book to fulfill that obligation. Not everybody can be a captain, a congressman, or a policeman, but those of you who have successfully made it into such a role should be held to a higher standard of behavior. You are expected to have more honor, more integrity, more discipline. You are expected to be more extraordinary than the "man on the street." If you are able to meet the challenges, then you should probably be prepared for some unexpected emotions to accumulate. Things like *time, effort, demands, restraints, disciplines, forethought, quick thinking,* and many others, were just not expected. At this point you will begin to feel some, if not all, of the following emotions:

- **Doubt** (I'm not sure if I will be able to handle this.)
- **Fear of the unknown** (I've never done anything like this before.)
- **Incapability** (I don't think I'm skilled enough for the task.)
- **Entrapment** (Look what I've gotten myself into.)
- **Discouragement** (Maybe I don't meet the criteria after all.)

Every leader was a potential leader first! An emotion is only a feeling and not a determiner. It should not be regarded as a counselor or a guide.

Be sure to "act" on your emotions and not "react." Your reactions can cause more damage than improvements. Your emotions are normal and every leader goes through at least one of these. You can't build a reputation on them, so why let them lead you? You will find that facing the challenge head-on is the best way to overcome it. There has never been a mountain overcome that was not climbed first. Everything the leader does is a challenge. If the challenges weren't met by him first, then he wasn't the leader, he was the follower.

What should be my code of conduct as a potential leader?

The leader should never get caught up in the "status quo." Sometimes the affairs of men get caught up in the same ol', same ol'. The leader is the one who is always looking for a new and better way to do things. Many complain that they keep getting the same results over and over again, when all they need to do is make a few changes. If they keep doing what they're doing, they're going to keep getting what they're getting. Second, you, as a leader, should do nothing for appreciation or praise. Leadership is not a reward. Many, many times, you will find that leadership is a thankless job. Keep these simple *principles* in mind as you progress through your potentiality:

- **Leadership is not a reward. It is a challenge.**
- **Leadership is *action*, not mediocrity.**
- **Leadership is vitality.**
- **Leaders progress (not to be confused with compromise).**
- **Communicate *effectively* with the people.**
- **Leadership is not a stepping stone or a destination. It is a journey.**
- **Work together, as a team! There is no "I" in "team."**
- **Leadership is not "superiority."**
- **Back your leader in all things.**

I often talk about principles. I consider myself "a man of principles." When *I do* or *do not*, it is because of the principles that govern me.

Principle can be defined as:

a. A rule or standard, especially of good behavior: *a man of principle.* **b.** The collectivity of moral or ethical standards or judgments.

The following *principles* should be found in every leader in order for him/her to be effective:

1) Be tactically professional.

Your thoughts and actions *must* be well thought-out. They will affect your potential if you are misunderstood. What you say and do can have positive or negative consequences.

I've served in municipal, state, and federal positions for more than twenty years. In that span of time, I have seen every example of the tactically unprofessional. There's nothing more disheartening than serving under a person that cannot deal with people in a manner that is tactically proficient. No person serving in a leadership position should have an inner circle of line staff, a clique, if you will. This is particularly damaging to the "leader's" reputation. When these type of things exist in departments, it becomes the subject of many misconstrued incidents and rumors.

2) Know your people and look out for their welfare.

It doesn't hurt any to be aware of your people's strengths and weaknesses. Armed with this information, you can have more of an impact on the individual. If you can have an impact on the individual, then you can impact the department. If you impact the department, then you impact the community. Do not utilize people in areas where they are not technically proficient. Look at their strengths, identify them, and utilize them in a manner that benefits the department and, ultimately, the public. Be conscientious of their people skills. If they cannot respect the people, they should probably be utilized elsewhere.

3) Keep the people informed.

Nothing brings more vexation than not knowing what all the labor is about. Nobody likes to be blindfolded. Share your ideas, reasons, goals, and outcomes. Then critique the mistakes, possible innovations, and be sure that new goals are set and understood. When you are engaging the community, tell them anything you are legally obliged to share. Be friendly with the public, and always remember, you are under oath.

4) Set the example.

The leader sets the standard of excellence. If you are in a mediocre mind-set, then your people are going to be mediocre. Show the people that you are a servant. In turn, they will learn to serve. Never ask the people to do something that you are not willing to do yourself. In my time of service, I've seen bad followers take up management roles and become anything but a leader. When this happens, the people have no respect for that person or that position. If you are in a position of a follower, fulfill that role to the best of your ability. Remember, people are always watching you, even when you are not in leadership positions; they watch you and take mental notes.

Most recently, I had the misfortune of working a staff position with an individual that earnestly coveted a leadership position that was already filled. Rather than letting this be his time to shine as a follower, he undermined his leader and actively sought to make him look bad to his employers. I'm sure his thought process was that eventually he would replace the man in charge as THE MAN IN CHARGE. He failed to set the example for those who worked with him directly and was eventually appointed to the position he sought, but not without a loss of respect from many of those who once worked with him, including yours truly. I resigned that position because I could not reconcile my unhappiness and lack of respect for the man with the job I needed to do. Don't forget that there will come a time when you will have to correct your subordinates, and they will bring to thought a laundry list of your shortcomings.

5) Ensure the task is understood, supervised, and accomplished.

A task will not be accomplished in the manner you have envisioned if you haven't shared it with the people. You must be able to communicate your vision in the language of the individual (know your people).

6) Train the people as a team.

Unity is not an automatic trait of the team. Unity must be forged. The team must learn to cast away such words as "I" and "me" and replace them with the words "us" and "we." Do not rely on one or two people in your department to take care of all the training. Seek to have every person fill a critical role so that the team can feel prolific. Unless you're in the military, do not publicly criticize. Team building is not the same in public service as it is in military service. There is no Uniform Code of Military Justice in the public sector. That being said, understand that there are repercussions for the way you deal with people. You can always be replaced, especially if you're serving in an elected or appointed position.

7) Develop a sense of responsibility and accountability in the people.

"Passing the buck" is unacceptable. It's an example that shouldn't be followed. You have to wonder how things in this world might have changed if the leaders in it would have taken responsibility for their own actions. A leader doesn't say to his people, "It's your fault." And the team shouldn't point fingers at one another either. If you, as a leader, are being criticized, don't turn the tables by criticizing the employee. Instead, inquire the reason you are being criticized, admit the fault, fix it, and carry on. If you cannot hold yourself accountable for your own shortcomings, don't expect others to take responsibility for their faults.

Nobody respects a "perfect" man, because only one has ever existed, and the rest are fictitious, except in your own self-image.

8) Use the people in accordance with their capabilities.

You don't want to give your people a task that they are not set to accomplish, or cannot accomplish. This could do damage to their conscience and/or confidence. Many times, early on, you may not know the capabilities of your people. In this case it will be necessary to search them out. When you are equipped with this knowledge, you will be able to properly use him/her in accordance with their capability. If your people are being used within their capabilities, there should be very few instances of damage control.

9) Seek responsibility and take responsibility for your actions.

As a leader, the people will look to you. Be sure to admit when you have made a mistake. There's nothing wrong with apologies. It's humble to apologize, and the people will admire that. A person who can admit his/her wrongs is a person that people can be comfortable around. As aforesaid, admit the fault and fix it. Remember you set the example!

"Nothing can stop the man with the right mental attitude from achieving his goal; nothing on earth can help the man with the wrong mental attitude."
—*THOMAS JEFFERSON*

Trait can be defined as a distinguishing feature, as of a person's character. A person's character will dictate traits necessary to be an effective oath keeper. These simple *traits* should be found in every leader:

1) Integrity: Uprightness of character.
"A man should be upright, not be kept upright." — *unknown*

There's no limit to what can be said about this trait. Integrity pretty much defines everything you do. It defines who you are, what you say, what you do, even what you think. The integrity that is ingrained within your character is the building block to all other principles of leadership. Integrity is something that should come pretty natural. It can be taught, but at no easy leisure. Your actions are a response to the way you think; therefore integrity ought to be at the root of everything you do.

"I cannot and will not recant anything, for to go against conscience is neither right nor safe. Here I stand, I can do no other, so help me God. Amen." — Martin Luther

Martin Luther was a man of integrity. In 1517, Luther pinned his ninety-five theses to the door of the Catholic Church. No matter what religion you are, you probably cannot deny that Luther had unwavering integrity. His conscience told him to act, and he acted. A person who chooses to ignore his conscience condemns his own integrity. A man's conscience will eventually become seared when he continually circumvents his integrity. Eventually, there comes a time when right and wrong is no longer considered, when the path of least resistance is optimal. The right path is not always the easy one to walk, but when you choose to take it, despite the opposition, your conscience will be clean and your integrity intact.

"Integrity without knowledge is weak and useless,

and knowledge without integrity is dangerous and dreadful." —Samuel Johnson

What good is integrity if you're at a crossroads and you don't have the knowledge to choose the right path? Samuel Johnson had it right. A person without knowledge may consider the possibility that right and wrong are fluid. We're commonly seeing this in American leadership; people with the inability to see evil as it is, or to call evil "evil."

Early in the Obama administration, Janet Napolitano, former homeland security secretary, refused to use the term "terrorist" or "terrorism," choosing instead to call them "extremists" and "man-caused disasters." Obama, after the Benghazi attack, failed to say "terrorists" or "terrorist attack," choosing instead to say, *"No acts of terror will ever shake the resolve of this great nation, alter that character, or eclipse the light of the values that we stand for,"* on September 12th, 2012. You may feel that it's just a play on words, but the reality is, Obama doesn't see in black and white; he sees everything in shades of gray. On September 12th, 2012, Obama appeared on *60 Minutes*. Obama was asked if he believed Benghazi was a terrorist attack.

Obama replied, **"Well, it's too early to know exactly how this came about, what group was involved, but obviously it was an attack on Americans. And we are going to be working with the Libyan government to make sure that we bring these folks to justice, one way or the other."** This may or may not be integrity, but it was certainly spoken without knowledge of right/wrong and good/evil.

2) Knowledge: Awareness or familiarity.
"In expanding the field of knowledge, we but increase the horizon of ignorance." —Henry Miller

The above quote is not necessarily a bad thing. What Miller was saying is that the more you learn, the more you understand you don't know that much. I realized that years ago one day while I was in deep thought. I would compare it to a library: you know what a library is, and you know what you're going in to read, but as you study the topic matter, you find yourself researching more than you had anticipated. New doors open with every minute of research. In short, you leave smarter, but feel overwhelmingly uneducated.

Being in a leadership position requires you to know that you don't know it all. That's why it's so important to surround yourself with knowledgeable people and numerous resources. When you don't know the answer to a question, let them know you don't have the answer, but you will get it.

"A little knowledge that acts is worth infinitely more than much knowledge that is idle." —Kahlil Gibran

To paraphrase, "work with what knowledge you have, not without it, and certainly don't let your knowledge go unused." If you have people working for you that are knowledgeable in any given area, utilize them. Like Ralph Cudworth stated: *"Knowledge is not a passion from without the mind, but an active exertion of the inward strength, vigor and power of the mind, displaying itself from within."*

3) Courage: Ability to disregard fear; bravery. *"Courage is a quality so necessary for maintaining virtue, that it is always respected, even when it is associated with vice." —Samuel Johnson*

I want to dispel the myth that *courage* is a lack of

fear. It's just the opposite of that. Courage is having fear but choosing to disregard it. This is something felt by most oath takers, especially those who put their own safety aside for the preservation of *liberty*. Our military men and women, our police, those who contract their services overseas, security guards; the list can go on, but the point has been made.

Leaders have a job which sometimes requires them to counsel those they work with. When doing this, you may feel apprehension due to the possibility of a confrontation. If this happens, you have two options; either disregard the apprehension, taking into consideration any other issues that need to be resolved, or disregard the possibility of a confrontation. These two options still require you to do so with knowledge and understanding. There sometimes needs to be contingencies in place in case there is a confrontation. Generally people become defensive, if the counseling is more severe. This can be neutralized by the way you approach the matter. Always talk about strengths before you attempt to resolve the shortcoming. After you have bolstered the person's character and delicately resolved the issues, you need to finish by complimenting the person on their strengths. If you have these things in mind at the time of the meeting, you will be focusing on positive things that tend to neutralize the negative and that will help push the element of fear or apprehension out of the equation. This system will work wherever courage is required, you will just need to alter the thought processes that take you into the moment of dread.

"Courage is not simply one of the virtues but the form of every virtue at the testing point, which means at the point of highest reality." —C.S. Lewis

In short, be brave when things are most difficult, and don't give up. Only through the fire can your bravery be tested.

4) Decisiveness: Quick to accurately decide.
"There is a time when we must firmly choose the course we will follow, or the relentless drift of events will make the decision." —Herbert V. Prochnow

Many oath taker duties require quick and

decisive action. In some lines of duty hesitation can get someone killed. God forbid, someone under your area of responsibility becomes the victim of your inaction. Sometimes, nature allows for deliberation, but other times its judgment is instant and forever settled.

"In every success story, you find someone has made a courageous decision." —Peter F. Drucker

5) Dependability: Reliable.
"The only way to make a man trustworthy is to trust him." —Henry Lewis Stimson

No employee will ever blossom beyond their current status of mediocrity if they're not empowered with responsibility. This is also a good opportunity to test a person's strengths and character.

Dependability is required of every leader. The people are watching to see if you are dependable, just as you are watching your leaders to see if they are dependable. In all things be faithful and watch your work ethic become renowned.

6) **Initiative:** The action of taking the

first and leading step.
"A lot of people never use their initiative because no-one told them to."
—Banksy

This is a very true and powerful statement. I have worked in environments where the employer does not want to be bothered with a hundred questions, but on the same note will bark frustrations at you for using initiative. I've always used initiative, even to the frustrations of my supervisor. I would rather seek their forgiveness than give my authority away along with the ability to make decisions on my own. I'm in a position of leadership; therefore I will utilize any and all traits associated with leadership.

7) Tact: Having the ability to avoid what would disturb somebody.
"Euphemisms are not, as many young people think, useless verbiage for that which can and should be said bluntly; they are like secret agents on a delicate mission, they must airily pass by a stinking mess with barely so much as a nod of the head, make their point of constructive criticism

and continue on in calm forbearance. Euphemisms are unpleasant truths wearing diplomatic cologne." —Quentin Crisp

I touched on this in the *courage* section of this chapter. I love the quote and Crisp delivered it proficiently tactfully. Leaders with no tact are generally not considered friendly people. Public speakers and PR officers need to be proficient in this trait. Be mindful that the words you choose can have a positive or negative outcome. Keep in mind that there are generally sects of people dissecting your words to reformulate them into an agenda of their own.

"Give thy thoughts no tongue, Nor any unproportioned thought his act. Be thou familiar but by no means vulgar." —William Shakespeare
"Tact is after all a kind of mind reading." —Sarah Orne Jewett

8) Justice: The principle of moral or ideal rightness.
"If we do not maintain Justice, Justice will not maintain us." —Francis Bacon
Justice has a way of policing itself. If the oath taker

cannot oblige himself/herself to honor their oath, then a series of unfortunate events are sure to follow. It takes great patience to rely on the American system of justice. Many times in my police work, officers are likely to spend countless hours on a case, just to see the State's attorney dismiss it. It's difficult to keep a positive attitude when justice isn't being served up by those who have sworn to uphold it. There was a point in my own career that I almost gave up entirely. Eventually I came to my senses and went back to work emboldened by the thought of getting my job done, even though there are individuals on the side of justice not doing theirs.

"Justice should not only be done, but should manifestly and undoubtedly be seen to be done." — Lord Hewart

> 9) **Enthusiasm:** Intense feeling for a cause.

"It's faith in something and enthusiasm for something that makes a life worth living."
—Oliver Wendell Holmes Sr.

Everybody wants to work for a cheerful and enthusiastic leader. Happy employees are productive employees; miserable employees will be poison in your bones! My lifelong goal as a leader was always to be fair, firm, and friendly across the board. Fair in judgment, firm in discipline, and friendly to all.

10) Bearing: Ability to maintain a proper attitude.
"Let the world know you as you are, not as you think you should be, because sooner or later, if you are posing, you will forget the pose, and then where are you?" —Fanny Brice

A couple things could be said about bearing. First, a proper and consistent attitude should always be maintained. If you are consistently in a positive state of mind, then your people will know when you are out of sorts. That's not necessarily a bad thing as long as you know you have lost your bearing. It becomes a bad thing when you have lost your bearing and you fail to notice it. Another way to say it, if you've lost your bearing, you've lost your way. Many oath takers have lost their way and have been misplaced on the road we call "duty."

Second, don't be a fake leader. Posing to be somebody you are not will eventually catch up with you. Some people confuse leadership with power and, in doing so, seek after the authority and fall into a position that requires leadership. I would like to think there is a fail-safe for these types of instances that would keep a power-grabber from attaining these goals, but unfortunately, unions have been set up in many organizations that provide equal opportunities for leaders and power-grabbers. Be sure your motives are pure when you set out for the position you are seeking. Leadership is a journey, not a destination.

11) Endurance: Ability to withstand prolonged strain.
"Life is truly known only to those who suffer, lose, endure adversity and stumble from defeat to defeat." —Ryszard Kapuscinski
"Sure I am of this, that you have only to endure to conquer. You have only to persevere to save yourselves." —Sir Winston Churchill

Endurance can easily go hand-in-hand with patience and long-suffering. No true leader can ever understand the need for perseverance in a person's life, if he has not endured, himself. Sometimes the process of developing into a leader requires your leader to make you wade through prolonged circumstances that require endurance. The way endurance is instilled in a leader is by subjective experiences with it while you are in a position of a follower.

12) Unselfishness: Unconcern for one's own interests or pleasures.

"That man is good who does good to others; if he suffers on account of the good he does, he is very good; if he suffers at the hands of those to whom he has done good, then his goodness is so great that it could be enhanced only by greater sufferings; and if he should die at their hands, his virtue can go no further: it is heroic, it is perfect." —Jean de La Bruyère

"And though I bestow all my goods to feed the poor, and though I give my body to be burned, and have not charity, it profiteth me nothing. Charity suffereth long, and is kind; charity envieth not; charity vaunteth not itself, is not puffed up." —

Apostle Paul

13) Loyalty: Faithfulness.
"A sense of duty is useful in work but offensive in personal relations. People wish to be liked, not to be endured with patient resignation." —*Bertrand Russell*

I enjoy being liked; most people do. When I go to work, I do not have a mind-set to make trouble wherever life may lead. Rather, I enjoy making people laugh and I take whatever route I can to get there, generally at the cost of a momentary loss of professionalism. But the thing that's great about loyalty is, the people that work for me laugh with me; then we get back to being professional.

14) Judgment: Discernment; good sense.
"A primary function of art and thought is to liberate the individual from the tyranny of his culture in the environmental sense and to permit him to stand beyond it in an autonomy of perception and judgment." —*Lionel Trilling*

Judgment isn't always the simple definition of

decision-making, whether good or bad. There's a deeper discernment involved that includes other faculties of the mind, involving wisdom, knowledge, and understanding. These three things need to be properly calculated into an entire picture of everything it's being applied to. It's much easier for a judge or a jury to collect evidence and sit and think on a situation and the decisions and actions that went into it than it is for an oath taker to make an instantaneous decision only with available information. That decision can be of extreme weight, which is why a leader must be equipped before he leads.

"Caution has its place, no doubt, but we cannot refuse our support to a serious venture which challenges the whole of the personality. If we oppose it, we are trying to suppress what is best in man—his daring and his aspirations. And should we succeed, we should only have stood in the way of that invaluable experience which might have given a meaning to life. What would have happened if Paul had allowed himself to be talked out of his journey to Damascus?" —Carl Jung

I tried my best to establish everything I could on the fundamentals of leadership. The bottom line is that leaders cannot be leaders without followers. Followers make leading possible, and leaders make following possible. It is a symbiotic relationship that cannot exist one without the other.

If you are an oath taker, mind your fundamentals of leadership as you uphold the Constitution of the United States of America. People will be closely monitoring you and your abilities to lead in times when governments are corrupt. Please don't get caught up following the crowd or going with the grain. Some of the most beautiful wood patterns I've seen contain grains that don't flow with the rest. It is the American spirit to stand against tyranny, not with it.

WE NEED YOUR SUPPORT, ARMY, NAVY, AIR FORCE & MARINES

"True patriotism sometimes requires of men to act exactly contrary, at one period, to that which it does at another, and the motive which impels them the desire to do right is precisely the same."
—Robert E. Lee

I'm going to write as frankly as possible. I haven't refrained from saying things the way I feel and I certainly believe the time for tiptoeing around in the tulips and walking on eggshells is long past.

Most people I speak with can sense that something is not right in this country, and others can sense that something bad is going to happen soon. When the conversations take off, there are several mass crisis events that are mentioned. However, the endgame is always the same: *the U.S. military.*

Let me attempt to put your mind at ease with a couple of my thought processes. First, to the nonmilitary Americans, the States are too big, and the population too large, for the military to contain a workable martial law. The U.S. government would rely heavily on the state, municipal and county law enforcement agencies to assist. Martial law includes the confiscation of oil fields, farms, water, power plants, etc. It is the oath taker that will be commanded by a tyrannical leader to seize these key resources. To the U.S. military Americans, you are governed by the Uniform Code of Military Justice. Every veteran has served under it and all active duty military men and women are serving under it. The orders your command gives you **cannot go against the UCMJ, nor can they be contradictory to the U.S. Constitution;** any such order is **unlawful**. If you are currently serving in the U.S. military, **you are obligated to oppose any unlawful order given to you or contrary to the U.S. Constitution.** Your command staff are very familiar with the UCMJ and understand perfectly well their obligations to ensure lawful obedience to it and to the Constitution. For your convenience, I am printing Article 90, for the sake of highlighting a couple truths.

Article 90 - UCMJ

Any person subject to this chapter who–

(1) strikes his superior commissioned officer or draws or lifts up any weapon or offers any violence against him while he is in the execution of his office; or

(2) willfully disobeys a lawful command of his superior commissioned officer;

shall be punished, if the offense is committed in time of war, by death or such other punishment as a court-martial may direct, and if the offense is committed at any other time, by such punishment, other than death, as a court-martial may direct (Article 90 Uniform Code of Military Justice).

First, Article 90, section 1 is very clear that you cannot strike a commissioned officer **while he is in the execution of his office**; and secondly, section 2 states that **you cannot willfully disobey a lawful command.** With these points highlighted, it's apparent that it is indeed lawful to disobey an unlawful order. The UCMJ protects you from willful disobedience if the commands are unlawful. Commanders, not only are you obliged to give lawful orders, but the UCMJ also protects servicemen and women who willfully disobey an unlawful order that you give. When it is determined that your orders are tyrannical and unconstitutional, the UCMJ says they are not committing mutiny, should they deem it necessary to purge their command of tyranny.

Article 94 – UCMJ

(a) Any person subject to this chapter who–

> *(1) with intent to usurp or override lawful military authority, refuses, in concert with any other person, to obey orders or otherwise do his duty or creates any violence or disturbance is guilty of mutiny;*
>
> *(2) with intent to cause the overthrow or destruction of lawful civil authority, creates, in concert with any other person, revolt, violence, or disturbance against that authority is guilty of sedition;*
>
> *(3) fails to do his utmost to prevent and suppress a mutiny or sedition*

being committed in his presence, or fails to take all reasonable means to inform his superior commissioned officer or commanding officer of a mutiny or sedition which he knows or has reason to believe is taking place, is guilty of a failure to suppress or report a mutiny or sedition.

Again, the key words are *lawful military authority* and *lawful civil authority*. If it is unlawful authority and/or unlawful civil authority in question, then the UCMJ does not apply.

I understand that there is not a single legitimate military person that desires to raise arms against another American. Your oath is to protect them; after all, you are one of them. The armed populace of the United States are the militia. They are the unorganized men and women who history used to help win the American Revolution. They are different from the military raised by Congress. The armed services of the United States are provided for through the government, but are not *of the government*.

You are, first and foremost, Americans, charged with the security of our country from threats, whether of foreign design or domestic tyranny. The

Bill of Rights provides each individual American with a right and an obligation to be at all times armed, in order to maintain a free state (*A well regulated militia, being necessary to the security of a free state, the right of the people to keep and bear arms, shall not be infringed*).

The Fourteenth Amendment ensures that no state can curtail their individual rights, especially those ensured by the Constitution. Many leftist politicians attempt to abridge rights not specifically mentioned in the Constitution, even though the Ninth Amendment protects rights not specified in the Constitution.

It is feared (by some...not me) that there will come a time when soldiers go door knocking for the purpose of gun collecting. Personally, I believe the Liberals have adopted a slow and methodical plan to erode the people's right to being armed. I am not expecting that door knock for registered weapons. Instead, I am watching as the government regulates the sales and registration of firearms. Both of which are infringing the people's Second Amendment.

I've said, time and again, that hard choices are to be made. Many things are not right in this country, and Thomas Jefferson masterfully stated,

"Whenever any form of government becomes destructive of these ends [life, liberty, and the pursuit of happiness] it is the right of the people to alter or abolish it, and to institute new government." The government has already grown to the point of being destructive to individual liberty. The Constitution simply does not give the government power to infringe upon sovereign individual liberties! The individual liberty is unique to each and is protected as such. *"Rightful liberty is unobstructed action according to our will within limits drawn around us by the equal rights of others. I do not add 'within the limits of the law' because law is often but the tyrant's will, and always so when it violates the rights of the individual."*

And so, looking into the mind of Thomas Jefferson, it's clear where his mind would be if he were alive today. He certainly wouldn't be aligned with a transitioning form of government. He didn't help design a government with socialist benchmarks. No, he helped design a republican form of government. One where the power resided with the people and the people were free to abolish government and rebuild it at will. He

assisted in the development of a country where the constituents can remain free and never debarred the use of guns: *"No freeman shall be debarred the use of arms."*

In short, the American people ought not to have the fear of its counterpart, the U.S. military, working in alignment with a tyrannical government to confiscate weapons. The U.S. military operates under the same Constitution that provides us the right to **keep** and **bear** arms. It also operates under a very strict set of codes that condones death, in some situations, to military members should they violate certain articles of the UCMJ.

No, sir, I do not fear the military. I am their brother, trained as they are trained, sworn as they are sworn, educated as they are educated, believe as they believe. In fact, I believe it is the government that should fear their own military, for they have sworn to defend against domestic tyranny. In a country where its government has grown too large, the elected should understand full well that its constituents are a people made up of veterans, trained warriors of all classes, military men and women, police officers, correctional guards, tough as nails firefighters, and the world's largest militia.

Here are two awesome quotes by Admiral Isoroku Yamamoto, commander in chief of the Japanese Imperial Navy, that I want to use out of context, in regards to WWII:

"You cannot invade the mainland United States. There would be a rifle behind each blade of grass." And, *"I fear all we have done is awaken a sleeping giant and fill him with a terrible resolve."*

The reason I find these quotes so awesome is there relevance for today. It's not a world war, or even an invasion, it's the thought of a high-minded commander in chief having enough wisdom to know what would be a stupid idea and his regret for having taken an alternate action. Not only are patriotic American people aware of the left's attempt at striking out a bill of individual rights, but they are armed to the teeth and full of terrible resolve. The most foolhardy thing this corrupt government could do is knock on doors for guns. Never underestimate American resolve and never forget we know exactly what you're trying to do. You're not pulling the wool over the watchful eyes of gun owners. Try, you may, but fail you will.

Sheriffs and police chiefs should have already considered where their alignment would be, should the winds change. I know the officers that I have spoken with have considered the possibility. I generally ask them the question, "Have you ever considered where your loyalties would be if the federal government asked you to aid them in a state of martial law?" So far, the responses have been unanimous. They are Americans first. With that mind-set, they know their position in law enforcement is not forever. At some point, you return to your life as a civilian, a civilian without a means to protect yourself. Don't be fooled into thinking the LEOSA bill will save you. There will be no end to gun confiscation, should it start.

The United Nations is constantly trying to disarm Americans and America's police departments. The recent terrorist attacks in England and France are good reasons to maintain an armed defense force. French and English police officers should be armed so that they can defend themselves. Never should any human be left to the mercies of an evildoer.

SOME FINAL THOUGHTS ON DEMOCRACY

"I hold it that a little rebellion now and then is a good thing, and as necessary in the political world as storms in the physical. Unsuccessful rebellions indeed generally establish the encroachments on the rights of the people which have produced them. An observation of this truth should render honest republican governors so mild in their punishment of rebellions, as not to discourage them too much. It is a medicine necessary for the sound health of government."
—Thomas Jefferson

"The spirit of resistance to government is so valuable on certain occasions, that I wish it to be always kept alive. It will often be exercised when wrong, but better so than not to be exercised at all. I like a little rebellion now and then. It is like a storm in the atmosphere."
—Thomas Jefferson

"The natural progress of things is for liberty to

yield, and government to gain ground."
—*Thomas Jefferson*

I've never been a fan of democracy. When a nation's generation becomes evil, the degradation of the country follows. The desires of the majority wins the day and the rest is a minority report. If a democracy is what you want, move to a country with a constitutional monarchy form of government, like Canada or Great Britain. These are good countries with a government where the majority of the people get to vote to determine the amount of interference they can have over the minorities. If you're the kind of person who feels a vote is in order to determine the rights of everybody else, you need to live in a democracy. America was not designed that way. Our Constitution is unique in the world. Nowhere else in the world is there a constitution as old or that provides sovereign rights to the individual the way ours does.

Ours is also unique in the right of the people to be armed for the purpose of maintaining a free state. Other countries have lost freedom and security and slipped into destruction through confiscation of guns by its government. America's uniqueness is hinged upon the patriot having a well-supplied gun cabinet and a family educated in the history of our country and countries without freedom. The future security of our country is built upon the foundation of gun owners, patriots, veterans, and various individuals sworn to defend it against all enemies, foreign and domestic.

THE COCKROACH THEORY

A few years back, I was having a conversation with one of my friends. That, in itself, was nothing unusual. I rather enjoy having these deep talks with him about leadership, the state of our country and the world. When we get to talking about leadership and discussing the examples of good and bad leaders, people's names generally come up. What made me laugh was my friend's notion that the dirtiest of players usually rise to the top. I can't remember which of us brought it up, but the "cream rises to the top" proverb was mentioned. I do remember that it was I who returned with "so does the fecal matter in a cesspool." Not to be calling anybody "fecal matter," but my point was that not necessarily is it a good or true proverb that the best rise to the top. My friend and I laughed about it; then he went on to explain to me the Cockroach Theory.

Cockroaches are filthy insects that are masters of self-preservation. They appear wherever filth can be found and usually where no light touches. Their existence is almost always under cover of darkness and they scatter when the light is put on them. It is said that cockroaches can survive in conditions that would bring certain extinction to all other carbon-based life forms. That being said, cockroaches can survive in the most unexpected of conditions. They thrive in the dark and lurk in places you can't necessarily see. You can tell where cockroaches might live, but won't know for sure until you see them. They don't work, but manage to function and survive in the filth of their environment, usually an environment created by its host. The only way to combat this type of vermin is to avoid it altogether by maintaining a state of vigilance. You keep the environment clean and free of clutter and other things that would lure the vermin. They are especially attracted to messiness and any clutter that can be used to conceal its presence. Where you find one, there will certainly be more. In real-life conditions, a messy state of affairs is especially attractive to individuals looking to get a foothold in any scenario.

In a workplace, a lack of true leadership creates a vacuum where any type of management is acceptable. In politics, a politician that is not held accountable for bad action or inaction creates a monster that thinks he/she can get away with anything. In matters of national security, inaction leads to a lack of fear and emboldens the enemy to act.

The Cockroach Theory teaches us that we must maintain due diligence in every aspect of our lives if we are to be free of the types of people that would take up the opportunity to seize life as we know it. These people live among us and are ever present, waiting for their moment.

Years ago, in a period of my early leadership development, I learned about the ten percent rule. It doesn't matter how strict the hiring process or how difficult you make the interviews, ten percent will always be the bad apples. They inevitably fall through the cracks. It's the ten percent that make the company look bad. They're the ones that tarnish a good and respectable image in an instant, even if that image took years of building and sacrifice to create. They're the ones that spread pessimism and disgruntlement to all the new employees of your organization. They cannot be silenced or eliminated, because they are pushing an ideal that will continue to thrive in the form of another ten percent.

The Cockroach Theory states that ideals of

pessimism will always exist and cannot be destroyed, but can be managed and controlled by vigilance and due diligence. Happy members of your organization will almost always be productive. Good leadership will minimize the effects of the ten percent by maintaining a clean and respectable organization. People will be less likely to heed the complaints of the few when they themselves are happy. The ten percent will not find a foothold in a healthy environment. You've heard the phrase "Misery loves company"? Well, the Cockroach Theory teaches that where there's one, there's two or more.

ADDENDUMS

Much has changed from the time this book was realized and put in writing. Political figures have resigned, some were replaced in elections, and many unfortunate events have taken place.

In light of all the publicity covering the Ferguson and NYC cases involving the use of lethal force by law enforcement officers, I thought it important to elaborate a bit on the substance and the lack thereof involved in the aforementioned topics.

From the time this book began to take shape in my mind, and through the actual writing process, I have diligently watched the news and wondered at how I should approach the issues. I was going to ignore them altogether and just keep them omitted from this book. But, as I thought on it, I came to understand that righteousness must endure. Righteousness, by nature, is passive. Sometimes, passiveness is very much necessary. Sometimes excessive attention on any given topic only prolongs and exacerbates the problem. This is why I chose not to go over redundant and rhetorical ideologues that are plaguing the news. Instead, I want to address the difficult road ahead. I will briefly touch on the event, but for no other reason than as a foundation.

LEADERSHIP IN DIFFICULT TIMES

I purposefully included an entire chapter on leadership because of the impact it could have on people. Nothing says "leader" stronger or louder than a person saying the right things at the right time. In dark times, a country needs leadership. The people need to know that things are going to be okay and that wounds can heal. It troubled me deeply when I recently heard our President, the NYC mayor, the attorney general, a so-called "Reverend," and other elected officials instigating, perpetuating, antagonizing, and just plain "stirring the pot" on matters of perceived racism. Instead of bringing divisions together, chasms were wedged open.

When a person runs for an elected office, he runs for a leadership position. Leadership is not built into the office. But it should be instilled in the office holder. If you are incapable of saying the right things in difficult times, you are not a leader. If you choose sides based on who is the most clamorous, you are not brave. If you are blind to truth and you uphold injustice, you are a tyrant. Regarding the evil known as ISIS, we need a President that will call evil by its name. Calling a leopard by any other name is deception. To defeat an enemy of freedom, you must call it by its name. ISIS is an Islamic terrorist group. It is a cancer that must be eradicated from the face of the earth. Ignoring evil's intentions only emboldens it and condones its spread.

PROFESSIONALISM IN DIFFICULT TIMES

Law enforcement officers can't deny the truth that difficult times are ahead. Despite the lack of evidence to prove race was a factor in the Ferguson and NYC cases, political ideologues with faces have pressed the issue, most likely to draw attention from the real issue: failed policies. Virtually all LE understand there are no racial motivators in the events that unfolded in late 2014. They were most likely made into racial anecdotes by racial antagonists. The facts revealed to grand juries did not uncover racial motivators. They revealed crimes that were being committed where the use of lethal force was lawful and necessary. On the night the grand jury revealed its decision, violence on an unprecedented scale ensued. "Peaceful protesters" shouted lines about "dead cops" and police cars were burned. Since then, two NYC police officers were assassinated while in the line of duty for no other reason than being police officers.

I understand what the criminal element is wanting. They want a lawless society where they can do what they want, without the bother of consequence. I say "bother" because I do not think there is "fear" of consequence. The element causing all the mayhem in these locations is not the popular opinion of the masses. They are out-of-town opportunists that are exploiting rifts in society to gain a foothold for selfish gain.

It is of the utmost importance that every sworn office understands that the time ahead will prove most difficult, not because your job is tough, but because you must differentiate and find balance between safety, security, and professionalism without losing yourself or your image. You must work more diligently to secure an image of fairness and professionalism because there are forces telling lies about you. You must prove them wrong while maintaining a secure environment. God forbid the day you have to use lethal force to save a life. A jury will deliberate for days on a decision that you had to make in a split second.

MINEFIELDS

My livelihood rests upon dependency upon subordinates and peers to function as a team. I spent some time talking to a co-worker recently about survivability in difficult and dangerous work environments. Sixteen years working directly with the mentally ill in a maximum security environment earns a person the right to be called a survivor. The co-worker, a registered nurse, explained to me his conversation with a relative about our work environment. He said, "It's kind of like a minefield; you never know when you're about to step onto something; and if you manage not to step on it, the person next to you may, and it can take you down with him." I said, "That's a really good analogy." In fact, it's the comment that inspired this subtitle.

Minefields are dangerous environments that sometimes you unwittingly wander into. Other times, you know you're in a minefield and your task is to dismantle them or avoid them altogether.

One of the environments in which I work absolutely refuses to specify details in policy/procedure. That gives the perception that the workplace has chosen not to specify so that when you are called out on the carpet for a bad decision, you cannot point back to policy.

There have been many instances of disciplinary actions taken against employees no matter which action they take. The cliché "You're damned if you do and damned if you don't" definitely applies. This type of policy/procedure keeps the employees most miserable and ensures a continued lack of progress. Unfortunately, without a change of administration, all you can do is try to avoid minefields. If you work in this type of environment, the best of luck to you.

EPILOGUE

The epilogue is an important piece of a book. This book was my first ever and was extremely difficult due to the sheer amount of thought and consistently changing data that was almost fluid in content. I want to be clear that the portions of this book that are absolute are the chapters dealing directly with the Constitution. I have tried my best to provide only true data and using quotes wherever possible. There was a constant flow of news during the rise of the Ferguson situation that was impossible to keep up with. When discussing the crisis of Ferguson and New York, I tried to include relevant information for the oath taker. The views expressed are my own and do not reflect the views of any editor, publisher, or participant in the publication of this book.

I withhold judgment as to whether or not they should be the views of every oath taker. I do understand that political views are expressed in this book, but I need the reader to understand they were stated because political opinions can have an effect on the oath, especially in today's America. Political views are subjective, but the Constitution is not. It is objective and written to be taken literally, not dissected or interpreted.

America is not in a good place. Elected leaders are not leading, and the appointed offices are governed by their agenda. The President is writing law, and Congress is letting it happen. Presidential leadership has failed, in an epic way, and the American people seem to be ignoring it, for whatever reason. Enough cannot be said about the importance of the contents of this book. The contents that were included in this work were included because of a mutual context. The wolves are growing bold and making a final push against *liberty*. Be strong...be courageous...and STAY FROSTY!

OATH TAKERS

ABOUT THE AUTHOR

PHOTO BY
DEVON WOOD PHOTOGRAPHY

L. Douglas Hogan is a U.S.M.C. veteran with over twenty years in public service. Among these are three years as a USMC anti-tank infantryman, one year as a Marine Corps Marksmanship Instructor, ten years as a part-time police officer, and seventeen years working in state government doing security work and supervision. He has been married over twenty years, has two children, and is faithful to his church, where he resides in southern Illinois, and has authored several post-apocalyptic fictions books.

Made in the USA
Columbia, SC
24 October 2024